# Your Life, Your Choice!

*Living Your Life on Purpose*

Dr. Haley Jones

Your Life, Your Choice! Living Your Life On Purpose © Haley Jones 2013

www.drhaleyjones.com

The moral rights of Haley Jones to be identified as the author of this work have been asserted in accordance with the Copyright Act 1968.

First published in Australia 2014 by Gowor International Publishing

www.goworinternationalpublishing.com

ISBN 978-0-9924977-0-5

Any opinions expressed in this work are exclusively those of the author and are not necessarily the views held or endorsed by Gowor International Publishing.

All rights reserved. No part of this publication may be reproduced or transmitted by any means, electronic, photocopying or otherwise, without prior written permission of the author.

**Disclaimer**

All the information, techniques, skills and concepts contained within this publication are of the nature of general comment only, and are not in any way recommended as individual advice. The intent is to offer a variety of information to provide a wider range of choices now and in the future, recognising that we all have widely diverse circumstances and viewpoints. Should any reader choose to make use of the information herein, this is their decision, and the author and publisher/s do not assume any responsibilities whatsoever under any conditions or circumstances. The author does not take responsibility for the business, financial, personal or other success, results or fulfilment upon the readers' decision to use this information. It is recommended that the reader obtain their own independent advice.

# Dedication

This book is dedicated to my maternal grandmother, Constance Ruth O'Shea (nee Read, 1921-1987), Nanny, who influenced my life in ways I am only just beginning to fully appreciate and fathom. I am truly inspired by her strength and courage in difficult circumstances, growing up in a time when education for women was deemed of little importance, and bringing up two children during the 1940s and 1950s, largely as a single parent working two or more mundane jobs when welfare was practically non-existent. Her greatest influence over me, however, was through her interest and practice in spirituality, and is, in large part, the reason this book ever came to be written.

# Contents

A Personal Note from the Publisher ................................................ ix

Foreword ................................................................................. xi

Introduction ............................................................................. 1

Chapter 1 – Where Are You and How Did You Get Here? ................ 5

Chapter 2 – What Does Your Happily Ever After Look Like? ........... 19

Chapter 3 – Creating a Fulfilling and Meaningful Life .................... 35

Chapter 4 – Escaping the Human Zoo ......................................... 49

Chapter 5 – What's Possible? ..................................................... 65

Chapter 6 – What is Your Passion? ............................................. 81

Chapter 7 – Intuition – The GPS for Your Life .............................. 95

Chapter 8 – Visualisation .......................................................... 109

Chapter 9 – Making The Transition ............................................ 121

Chapter 10 – Developing A Business Plan ................................... 133

Chapter 11 – Living Your Passion Now ....................................... 147

Chapter 12 – Seeing It Through ................................................. 161

Conclusion .............................................................................. 179

Acknowledgments .................................................................... 181

About The Author .................................................................... 183

# A Personal Note from the Publisher

To the reader,

As the Founder of Gowor International Publishing, my publishing company, I make it part of my practice to offer a personal review for my Authors about their book. The reason why I do this is so that YOU, as the reader, can glean a further understanding into why this book is so valuable to you in your life.

Ever since I met Haley in late 2012 – the beginning of her journey to become an author – I have been impressed with her persistence in helping people to live the life of their choice, as the title of this book suggests. Haley truly believes in people's potential to make grounded, real changes in their life so that their existence is more meaningful than a 9-5 job or our obligations and responsibilities in this world.

Haley's gift to you in this book is that she only presents the concepts to you that she *knows* work. You won't read anything in these pages that hasn't been through Haley's filter of healthy scepticism – leaving you with the perfect blend of deep wisdom, exercises and guidance that actually work, and of course, her love.

You will feel Haley's conviction on every page of this carefully-crafted book, and I am certain that it will inspire you to choose a life instead of living the one you were handed. It's time to go beyond what you know as familiar and step into the realm of possibility that Haley invites you into through every chapter of *Your Life, Your Choice!*

With inspiration,

Emily Gowor
Founder of Gowor International Publishing

# Foreword

by Angela Hryniuk

We, as a species, according to Buddhism, are in the midst of a Kali Yuga, an Age of Degeneration and darkness. In a Kali Yuga, we witness an increase in violence worldwide, the rise of child sexual promiscuity and early sexual development, and environmental disasters: tsunamis, fires, cyclones. Basically, it is a downward spiral of humanity. Just at the nadir of the destruction, the planet experiences a re-birth, a period of extreme light. It is at this time when new prophets and Divine beings arrive.

Dr. Haley Jones's book, *Your Life, Your Choice! Living Your Life on Purpose*, is being birthed into the world at a time when her message is not only welcomed, but necessary. People from all walks of life are beginning to turn inwardly for answers, realising there is no longer any external authority to one's own life. The good news is: if people are on a diligent spiritual path, their lives will increase in positivity, strength and abundance.

*Your Life, Your Choice!* takes the reader on a tremendous journey of "self-discovery", rather like a flashlight illuminating those parts about the self that heretofore may not have been "seen". Dr. Jones's thesis is in the title of the book; we have *choice* in life and we are here to *create meaning* and *have purpose* as we walk through the nearly 30,000 days (based on an 80 year life span) we have on this planet.

All of us will have faced times of deep despair, rejection, abandonment, hurt, resentment and jealousy. We will all have experienced the higher emotions of harmony, joy, calmness and peace. Even if fleetingly. However, no secular guidebook was ever given out for us to understand or make sense of all our emotions. If we were lucky, we may have had an elder in our life who pointed to deeper wisdoms.

There isn't a human being alive who doesn't aspire to be happy. Truly that is all anyone ever wants. Yet it is the most elusive, short-lived state of being for most people.

I have had the great fortune and privilege to spend many days working in the direct company of some of the world's finest Spiritual leaders, and Nobel Peace Prize Winners: His Holiness the Dalai Lama, Bishop Desmond Tutu, and Shirin Ebadi. People who are happy, by choice.

These giant world leaders have endured great human hardships, from imprisonment as a judge fighting for human rights in Iran, in Shirin Ebadi's case; challenging systemic racism in the apartheid system in South Africa in Bishop Tutu's life; and being exiled from his Tibetan home to a foreign country for the majority of his life, in His Holiness' case. They've all had both personal and political enemies who were outspoken against their beliefs, yet each of them not only endured the suffering, but have actually triumphed into greater human beings.

Being in the "Presence" of such luminaries, I couldn't help but be humbled firstly by their vast and extensive knowledge, then by their compassion, and finally by their humility. They chose how they felt about their oppressors, as their circumstances were non-negotiable. They chose to be empowered by their adversity rather than be defeated.

I, too, have overcome many of life's most difficult obstacles: violence, abuse, and neglect in my childhood, then years in active addiction, to be followed by nearly two decades of sobriety. I have seen my fair share of psychiatrists and therapists throughout my half century on the earth, and changed countries to finally come to a place of internal wholeness and peace. I have sat for many thousands of hours in meditation, on retreat, on ground both east and west. I've had the great good fortune to take teachings with the Dalai Lama on many, many occasions over the past 24 years as a Buddhist practitioner and teacher, worked with the United Nations, and dined with the President of India, as well as organized the Dalai Lama's 2004 Spiritual Teaching in Vancouver to 13,000 people.

I met Dr. Jones (I know her as Haley), while leading an Interfaith Buddhist Pilgrimage to India, in which she participated in December of 2013. A woman who I didn't know, who came out of the blue into my bubble, a PhD in engineering, no less, who wanted to join on a Spiritual Journey, emailed me one day. I interviewed her before saying yes, to find out how serious a practitioner she was. When she said she'd sat a few 10 day Vipassana retreats, and had a steady meditation practice, coupled with an assuredness and confidence in her voice, I said yes.

I was impressed with her practical questions and her willingness to be open to all experiences that were about to come her way. Although Dr. Jones was an unknown person to me and the group, she "fit right in" from the very start. I loved her curiosity, her intelligence, her open mindedness and willingness.

The initial intention was for our group to take teachings with the Dalai Lama in the Himalayas. However, because of His ill health, the teachings were cancelled. Despite that hiccup in our program, our group, including Dr. Jones, had private meetings and teachings with various Buddhist Enlightened sages in the South and North of India. We ventured to the actual spots the Buddha had meditated, attained enlightenment, and taught. In Dharmsala we had a private dinner with the Head of the Tibetan Archives and Library, who was formerly His Holiness's personal translator for the past 16 years and is a long time friend of mine.

Throughout our arduous spiritual journey Haley never seemed to flinch. She was steady in her emotional as well as spiritual capacities. There were a few confronting situations, as could have been expected, and Haley dealt with each maturely and magnanimously. Basically, Dr. Jones "walked the talk" of what has been written in these pages. She doesn't just write about lofty spiritual concepts and practices; I was witness to her daily life and interactions in the spiritual and mundane worlds of India.

When we met I had no idea Haley had written a book, THIS book, in fact. She had already outlined various stages of human development, which she herself had undergone. She had already asked herself THE BIG QUESTIONS about life purpose, hopes, dreams, and aspirations. She had already found teachers, mentors, and therapists, with whom she had taken herself back through childhood trauma, old belief systems and patterns. She had found out about human needs in general, then learned how to meet them herself.

Not only had she broken through the academic "pink" ceiling of post graduate studies to gain a PhD and become a fully-fledged academic, lecturing and researching in engineering, she had already gone into the deeper territory of meditation, calming the mind, confronting resistance, fear, and how to tap into her own passions and intuition.

When I met her, Dr. Jones had already found out about the importance of visualization, something Buddhists have been doing for over 2500 years, and she already knew how to "ferret out" her subconscious expectations bringing them into consciousness. To top it all off, she already had done work on financial freedom, networking and even business planning in order to live her Passion NOW. Phew. That was a lot of work to have accomplished.

And accomplished Dr. Haley Jones is.

This book is living proof of all the internal obstacles, and struggles she has overcome in order to provide credible guidance to you, the reader. One cannot write a book with such specific topics as *What is Really Going to Make You Happy*, and *Intuitive Response Versus Emotional Response*, without having rightfully transformed much delusional thinking and "poisons" of the mind. As a result of her experiences, she is able to bring to the planet a beautifully rendered, thoughtful, compassionate, and clear guide on how to do this same work for yourself. That is the book you are holding in your hands right now.

What is startling and refreshing about *Your Life, Your Choice* is that Dr. Jones not only offers wisdom and teachings from her own personal development, but she has integrated the teachings deeply. From this depth she guides and teaches new readers in very practical ways, offering specific techniques, practices and steps to turn one's life around, through to the process of "Becoming".

I love Dr. Jones's concept that we're really all "living in a zoo". In Buddhism we say that each of us lives in a prison, which is our own minds, and of our own creation. Haley's further extension of including the environment in which we live, as well as our own minds, further elucidates and accentuates the truth that we are truly Creating our Own Reality – living the life of our choice.

Life is "tricky business" is a statement within *Your Life, Your Choice* that really resonated for me both as a spiritual teacher, and a Buddhist practitioner. As soon as you think you've got something "licked" or "perfected", the Universe then ups the ante, and stretches us one step further into our "Greatness" by giving us more challenges and opportunities for growth.

What is also remarkable is that Dr. Jones comes from a more rational, technological and scientific background, arriving at spiritual answers to life's most complicated questions. This in itself is unusual and a feat. She has devoted her life to the sciences, yet her spirit has also called her to sacred practices. In this book we meet both Dr. Jones, the fiercely intellectual teacher, as well as Haley, the spiritual friend with a compassionate heart, the *kalyanamitra* that we can trust.

Her crisp, clear writing, her light hearted, encouraging and sometimes humorous tone encourages readers to take those initial steps onto the path of empowerment, individuation and magnificence. It will be a volume that will keep people delving deeply into themselves as they twist out of their old belief systems, transforming into new, greater versions of themselves. *Your Life, Your Choice* is a must have on every beginner's shelf.

You and I, Haley and His Holiness all share the same human emotions. We share the same human capacities and potential to bring meaning and purpose to our lives. It truly is <u>Our Life</u> and it is <u>Our Choice</u> as to how we want to live, and whether we choose to be happy or not; whether we choose to thrive or not. It IS our Choice. We need community, guides, texts, mentors and teachers to help us make better choices. They are always there to meet us, however, when the time comes for us to change.

In the long lineage of writers of historic wisdom, Krishnamurti, Kahil Gibran, St. Teresa of Avila, and then more in the contemporary tradition, Eckhart Tolle, Dr. Maya Angelou, Dr. Deepak Chopra, and Dr. Wayne Dwyer, Dr. Haley Jones is joining illustrious company, and she is rightfully placed.

As Dr. Jones's spiritual friend, her *kalyanamitra*, I am pleased and honoured to introduce *Your Life, Your Choice* to you, the reader. Enjoy the journey – it begins with one small step forward. Today. You have a great guide in your hands.

Angela Hryniuk, M.A.
Brisbane
June, 2014

# Introduction

Do you leap out of bed every day, excited at what lies ahead – even on Mondays? Do you bound from bedroom to bathroom to kitchen to the front door to get out and get on with the day because you know you're going to be doing something that you love? Do you have unlimited energy and enthusiasm for life because you've always got an exciting project on the go? Do people flock to you for your services because they love what you do as much as you do? Do you have all the material wealth you could ever hope for and travel to exotic locations on a whim?

Or, does the following sound more like you? Do you drag yourself out of bed every day – especially on Mondays – to force yourself to a job you are bored with at best, hate at worst? Do you yell at your kids/cat/spouse for no particular reason except that you're stressed and unhappy with the world and your lot in it? Do you feel stuck in a rut, caught in the rat race because you've got bills that just keep on coming and a mortgage to pay and have no idea how to change this?

If you answered "No" to any of the questions in the first paragraph and "Yes" to any of the questions in the second paragraph, then this book is for you! What you're going to learn in this book is that what's in your life, what your life looks like, is completely up to you. That's right – it's your life, your choice!

To me, doing something that you love is what life is all about. If you don't love what you do and aren't having fun most of the time (I'll allow that having fun ALL of the time is probably a bit unrealistic and, actually, not even desirable for personal growth), then there is room for change. You may even already know that. What you may not know is *how* you can change. After all, you've spent years cultivating particular habits and attitudes that have led you to where you are. Years of cultivation can't be uncultivated overnight – especially if you're not even aware that you've been cultivating, let alone what you've cultivated!

Unfortunately, though, if you try to leap from where you are to something like the description in the first paragraph, the chances are that you will become overwhelmed, overcome, and disillusioned and you will give up before you're even halfway there. I've been to many seminars where they talk about leaping – I've seen very few people who actually make it happen. For those who do, my belief is that they were already a lot closer than halfway there and actually just needed that push to get them over that last couple of miles.

Changing your life in a drastic way is not a sprint; it is, instead, very much like running a marathon. It's not impossible, but you have to prepare and train steadily for quite some time to condition yourself for the task, taking appropriate steps and consistent action to reach your goal.

So, for those of you who are a little bit further than a couple of miles out from the marathon finish line of such a life, this book is a conditioning manual for making real and lasting changes in your life. It provides you with the tools to help you to bridge the gap between where you are and where you want to be, that go beyond a bit of Ra, Ra, Ra! and taking a leap of faith.

So, why, I hear you asking, should you listen to me? In a nutshell, I know the personal development arena inside out. I have been studying personal development for many, many years, attending seminars, reading books and listening to tapes (yes, they were tapes back then!). They have ranged from the very spiritual (*A Course in Miracles* and *The Power of Now*), to psychology-based (*Emotional Intelligence* and *The Road Less Travelled*), to practical wealth-specific manuals (*Rich Dad, Poor Dad*) to pure "leap of faith" material such as the Abraham-Hicks books. In all I have spent well over $100K on personal development and wealth creation material and products, including $50K on just one course.

The choices I have made in my life have certainly been influenced by all of this material and my life has been enriched by the ideas I have met. However, I still come up against the ideas that were implanted in my head as a child that dictate what the most familiar and, therefore, comfortable (mentally, if not physically) life is for me, that make it difficult to change. Some of these ideas might sound familiar to you, too – "we can't afford that" or "you don't need a new car every two years" (unspoken implication – "you don't need to have enough money to afford a new car every two years") or "life is a struggle, your only hope is to plod along in your boring 9-5 job until you retire and then die". These ideas might have been explicitly said to you or else they may have just been implied by what you observed of the people around you – your family, your friends' families, and your neighbours.

As time went on and the untold riches still weren't landing in my lap (or my bank account), and I wasn't leaping out of bed with anticipation every or, actually, any day, I had to sit down and ponder what was going on. I decided that it wasn't the quality of the information I had found. By and large, the personal development material I had come across – seminars, tapes, books – was all of high quality. They generally contained many great ideas and suggestions. I also realised that some – those that really focus on mindset – had, indeed, helped me to make some small and some not-so-small changes in my life. But I still wasn't happy and the money wasn't rolling in. So what was missing?

I finally worked out that the key is knowing what is really important to you, what really excites you. I also realised that this is not necessarily something that you can work out in an instant – and probably not under pressure in a room full of Ra, Ra, Ra'ing strangers. Unless you've consistently taken the time to sit quietly and reflect on what is truly important to you, what you truly want in your life, deep down in your soul, you are most likely simply doing what you think you should be doing. And by what you think you should be doing, I mean what you perceive that others – your parents, your friends, society in general – think you should be doing. And this comes back to those ideas that were implanted in your head as a child.

Most of us do not take the time to reflect on anything beyond what to have for dinner. We get caught up in the busyness of life, plodding along on autopilot. We might go to a seminar and hear some great ideas that get us excited for a day or two, but when we get back to "real life" the auto-pilot gets switched back on again. And one of the reasons for this is that we think that we have to have the perfect new life mapped out in our heads before we can even get started. After all, how otherwise will you know what action you need to take to achieve your perfect life? And this is scary and overwhelming; after all, what if you get it *wrong*?!

Well, I've discovered that it is impossible to get it wrong. The personal development path is a journey, where a destination is never reached, but many brilliant, intriguing, wonderful places are visited along the way. If you can just start to visualise your life in this way, you will be well on the way to creating a compelling, wonderful life. So, reflect on what is important to you, what you'd like to have in your life and, when you find something that appeals to you, start taking action towards that.

You may have noticed the picture on the cover of this book. Yes, that is me skydiving. Let me assure you, that this is not a common pastime for me. I am not what you would call an adventurous person – not when it comes to doing activities that will end in almost certain death if something goes wrong. That is just not my style. However, part of the personal growth journey is about testing yourself, facing your fears and getting out of your comfort zone. With all of the personal development work that I have done and the amazing people that I have met and been influenced by, I just got to the point where I really wanted to try something that would scare the hell out of me but that I knew I would feel great about having done afterwards.

Who of us wouldn't love to be able to fly? We can all imagine how great it would feel. So, I did – literally – choose to take a leap of faith – out of an airplane. I was very nervous, but I decided I was going to enjoy it; otherwise, there was no point. And I did enjoy it. Every time I look at that photo and take a minute to remember and reflect on the experience, I feel a great swelling of pride. I remember how great it felt, and it reminds me that I did something that I was afraid of – and I survived; even thrived.

As you start moving towards your ideal life, your ideas will develop through your experiences and further reflection. You'll discover some things that you do like about what you've decided to do, some things you don't, and other things that you think will make it better. You might even discover something completely new that you hadn't considered previously, give away your first idea altogether, and start on a whole new path! And that's okay. You'll know you're on the right path because you'll be feeling happier and excited more of the time.

So, in this book, I will not be suggesting that you set outrageous leap-of-faith goals but, rather, that you first understand who you are and what is really important to you. Your goals will come naturally from what you discover and will be all the more readily achievable because they are intimately related to what is important to you. Rather than implicitly being about goals, then, this book is about discovering your purpose, whence your goals – and your fabulous, exciting and wealthy – if that's what you want – life will naturally unfold.

# Chapter 1

# Where Are You and How Did You Get Here?

*"Accept responsibility for your life. Know that it is you who will get you where you want to go, no one else."*

LES BROWN

In many personal development or self-help programs, there is an inclination to rush straight into "setting goals". They are usually big ones and often around the accumulation of stuff or material possessions, such as a fancy car or house. You are encouraged to "think big". You may be encouraged to set goals for each "area" of your life, such as health, fitness, wealth, where you live and what you live in, what car you want to drive and what experiences you want to have (e.g. skydiving or visiting an Indian ashram). You may also then be asked to divide them up into short-term (1 year), medium-term (3 years) and long-term (10 years) goals.

The notion behind this is that if you let your imagination run wild and become revved up enough, some of these goals might actually be accomplished one day. Once you accomplish one or two of them, you will have the confidence to try for more and you will keep achieving goals. You'll have the feted "abundant life" and you'll live happily ever after. Depending on how well you understand yourself and your dreams, there are many merits to this approach. However, if you are still struggling with the question of "what do I want to be when I grow up" then this approach can be frustrating and can leave you feeling empty.

Now, I want you to pretend for a minute that you have gone through this goal-setting exercise and that one of your goals is to be able to afford, and buy yourself, a specific really nice watch (if a watch isn't really your thing, replace the watch with a car or a yacht or some other material possession that appeals to you). Maybe it's a diamond-encrusted Cartier or a sleek Rado. Now ask yourself, what is the real meaning you have attached to having this watch? What is the real pleasure that you would get from owning this watch and how long will the pleasure last? Is it appreciating the excellence in workmanship and design? Is it having a better watch than your neighbour or that annoying guy at work, so it's the one-upmanship that pleases you? Is it simply the satisfaction of setting and achieving a challenging goal and not the watch at all? Or is it just knowing that you can afford it, so it's the wealth not the watch that gives you pleasure?

If it is the wealth, this would open up a whole new line of questioning. What is it about having wealth that appeals to you? Is it that you can now help and serve many people? Is it that you can now afford many other material things? Is it that you have the freedom to sit back and take the time to work out what it is that you really want in your life without being distracted by earning a living? Or is it something else? There is no right or wrong answer here. The purpose of asking all of these questions is simply to start you thinking about what is really driving you and how you really feel about the answer that you came up with.

The next step is to consider what has influenced your answers. Where are they really coming from? Are they coming from your heart? These are not always easy questions to answer. When you are sure that your answers to questions such as those in the previous paragraphs are, indeed, coming from your heart, then you are well on your way to understanding yourself and your life's purpose. I do not believe it is possible, nor desirable, to fully know your life's purpose, nor the exact path you should take, as new possibilities come before us as we grow and obtain greater understanding, knowledge, and awareness of both ourselves and the workings and possibilities of the world around us.

In this chapter you're going to start forming meaningful answers to these questions. You're going to be an observer and reflect on what has been in your life so far. What has worked and what hasn't? What is working, now, and what isn't? What do you want more of and what do you want less of? What haven't you tried that you've always wanted to try, even just once (e.g. bungee jumping or volunteer work). What haven't you tried that seems appealing? What kind of person do you want to be? Is there someone in the public eye, or a book or movie character that appeals to you, who you could aspire to be like?

## How Does Your Life Stack Up to Your Hopes and Dreams?

What is your view of life? Does life *happen* to you, or does it *flow* for you? Do you look forward to each day with an expectation of the great things you are going to create, or do you wake up dreading what might be in store? Your attitude to life has an enormous influence on how happy and fulfilled you feel you are – and how well you feel it stacks up to your hopes and dreams. In fact it has everything to do with how happy you are and it is one thing that you have complete control over.

The simplest way to change your attitude or how you feel is to think of something/someone towards which you have the attitude that you'd like to have instead, or something/someone that makes you feel the way you'd like to feel. For me, when I want to feel happier, I think of my nephews and nieces, the funny things they do and say and how grateful I am to have them in my life. Or I think of the love of my life and how grateful I am for having him in my life and for being able to feel the way I do about him and knowing that he feels the same way about me.

For most of us it is likely to be the people in our lives who make us the happiest or that have given us our happiest memories to draw upon, although it doesn't have to be people. It could be something you've achieved – maybe you got the top mark in your class in grade 7 for a science test, or you won the high jump at your school sports day in year 9. Or perhaps the memory of the football/netball/hockey team you follow winning the grand final one year can pep you up a bit.

Actually, my sister and her husband, not huge Australian Rules Football (AFL) followers, managed to choose the AFL grand final day for their wedding in 1997. They got married in Adelaide and the Adelaide Crows had made it to the grand final for the first time. Driving from my parents' house, far north of the city, to the wedding venue, more than an hour's drive away, far south of the city, there wasn't another soul on the roads – except for another football-ambivalent bride who was going the other way. So we waved at her.

The photographer was in his car, driving along next to us, and kept making hand signals at us along the way so we could keep up with the score. Unfortunately I had no idea what his hand signal meant, but one of the other bridesmaids had grown up in a football family, so caught on immediately. This created a really nice sense of camaraderie. Also, needless to say, many of the (male) wedding guests had "hidden" ear phones in their ears during the ceremony.

Happily, the Crows did win. It makes me smile to think of the wedding – and the football win.

Now you try it. Bring up a happy memory and focus on it for about a minute. Think about why it made you happy. Smile. Let yourself be immersed in the feelings you felt at that time. Now, in this state of mind, continue reading!

So, back to your life. Where are you? Is it where you want to be? These are pretty big questions. It is useful to consider them with respect to your life overall. ("How happy are you?" is basically what it boils down to.) However, it is also useful to consider them with respect to different aspects of your life, such as health, fitness, wealth/finance, fun, intimate relationship, family, friendships, and so on.

## *Pause for Thought #1: Where Are You Now?*

While reading about theory and other people's stories can be insightful for understanding yourself, I have always found self-reflection to be the most effective way to get to the bottom of, and begin to eradicate, any deep-rooted issues you may have. And, trust me, we all have them – some of us are just more aware of them than others. (And some people are excellent at being aware of others' issues and not their own, but I'm sure this isn't you!)

So, to help you to begin to address some of your emotional "stuff" – even, and especially, if you're not aware that you have any - I've included many *Pause for Thought* reflection exercises for you to start really diving deep into what makes you tick. The *Pause for Thoughts* consist of a number of questions related to the material you will have just read. There are no right or wrong answers, and many are somewhat open-ended. This is to allow you to fully and deeply reflect on your individual circumstances and experiences without being influenced by any assumptions that I might make about what insights or realisations you are likely to come to. As you work your way through them, you will start to notice some themes and patterns. Different *Pause for Thoughts* will trigger different memories and realisations that may lead you to go back to previous *Pause for Thought* exercises to update your answers with more details and insights.

Ideally, you'll have a quiet place to work on these exercises where you won't be disturbed for a while (at least 15 minutes, more if you can manage it). You'll have some paper to write on or a notebook to write in (preferably at least A4 or letter size – more space on the page gives your mind more space to wander and be creative) and a pen or pencil to write with. So, let's get stuck into your first *Pause for Thought* reflection.

| Life Area | Score/10 |
|---|---|
| Health | 6.5 |
| Career | 4 |
| Relationship | 7 |
| Fitness | 4 |
| Wealth | 5 |

Table 1: Example of Scoring Life Areas Out of 10

Choose at least 8 life areas to get a detailed enough picture of your life and write them down, one per line, as shown in Table 1. I suggest you don't choose more than 12, as it can become overwhelming, which is counterproductive. Having said that, you should choose as many life areas as you are comfortable with. Some examples include: health, fitness, wealth/finance, fun, intimate relationship, family, friendships, and so on.

- Give each life area a score out of 10, indicating how satisfied you are with that area of your life. A score of 1 indicates "not at all satisfied", and a score of 10 indicates "completely satisfied".
- What do you notice? Are there any areas with which you're particularly happy, having given yourself a 9 or a 10?
- Are there any areas for which you have given yourself 5 or less?
- Were there any surprises?
- When you consider all of your answers together, can you see any themes emerging? For example, are all of your relationships in disarray, or are you particularly pleased with your physical well-being?

There are many ways in which you could use this information. You could choose to focus on those areas in which you are already doing well, say having given yourself 8 or above, and decide that you are going to develop them all to a 10. You could, instead, choose to focus on those areas of your life that you didn't score yourself so well in, say 5 or less, and decide that you're going to develop those to at least a 7 in the next 3 months. You could choose one of the top ones and one of the bottom ones to focus on at the same time. That way you would have something that you're already feeling good about that you get to really focus on and become excellent at. Then, this will give you the strength of positive feelings required to help you to bring up the level of satisfaction of the lesser-scoring area.

The previous exercise looks at the standard areas of your life at a fairly surface level. Often, what is psychologically affecting one area of your life is also affecting other areas of your life or, almost certainly, all areas of your life. To really make this an in-depth, multi-level look at your life, you can also do this exercise at a more abstract level. You are now going to determine your satisfaction with various behavioural areas such as discipline, persistence, attitude, contribution, personal growth, connection with others, adventurousness, and so on.

When choosing behaviours for this part of the exercise, use terms that are positive; for example, "discipline" rather than "procrastination". Focussing on a positive behaviour and making it even stronger generates even more positive feelings and likelihood of success and can often eradicate a related negative behaviour without thinking about it. For example, focussing on being disciplined can eradicate procrastination because being disciplined naturally ensures that you do what you need to do, when you need to do it.

- As with the previous exercise, write down 8 to 12 different behavioural areas, such as those mentioned, or others of your own choosing that are more relevant or meaningful to you, and give them a score out of 10 for how they show up in your life.
- Now, go back to the previous set of questions and answer them for these behavioural areas. Again, when you are finished, choose one or two to focus on improving over the next 3 months.

## What Was Your Starting Point?

From the time you were a baby, you soaked up information and lessons from the people around you – your parents, grandparents, other relatives, and their friends. You took in what they did, what they said, and how they did and said it. And, you *missed out* on the things they didn't do and say. Those things were not a part of your world, not a part of your learning, so you didn't get the opportunity to take them in and integrate them as a part of your world. For example, someone born in the 17th century would have had no concept, let alone experience, of television, which most of us born since the 1940s take for granted.

From my own experience, I had no idea that such a thing as an avocado existed until I went to university, because my family couldn't afford such things when I was growing up. I had no concept of so-called "squat" toilets (which are much healthier for us than the throne-like ones we have in the West) until my family went to live in Malaysia for two years when I was eleven, when my dad was posted there with the Royal Australian Air Force.

So, as a child you grew up with certain expectations, based on your world experience and influences. While there are exceptions, more often than not, a child whose parents are working-class will grow up to have working-class values and a working-class lifestyle; a child who grows up in a middle class family will grow up with middle class values and matching lifestyle, and so on. The reason for this is that humans are *modellers*. You can see this in babies as soon as they start to notice things and have some control over their limbs and actions. They are miniature copycats! They don't want to be treated like a "child", they want to be treated like a person.

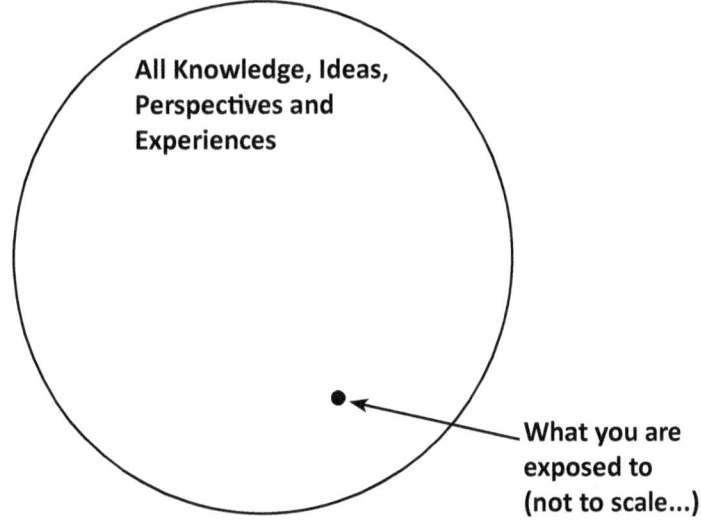

Figure 1: You experience only a small amount of what the world has to offer. If you didn't, you'd probably go insane with information overload!

As little people, they want to do the same things that the big people are doing because they assume that if the big people are doing it, it must be what people are supposed to do, regardless of their stature. And it is their natural instinct to want to fit in. It makes a lot of sense from a survival point of view. For big people to have gotten past the little people phase, they must have had some survival skills. So, it needs to be instinctual for a little person to want to be like a big person, so that they, too, can survive.

When my nephew was two, he was throwing a ball around the yard and particularly aiming it at plants and bushes. I guess he enjoyed that he got a reaction from them in terms of movement when the ball hit. I told him that he shouldn't throw it at the bushes and went up to the bush and stroked it, saying "poor bush," so that he would get the idea. He immediately went up to the bush and stroked it himself, saying "poor bush." Then he threw the ball at it again. So, he didn't understand my words, but he did copy my actions!

Based on your experiences and influences growing up, then, you have certain expectations for how your life should be and what you should be able to achieve. And you make decisions based on these expectations. Your life, at any particular point in time, is a culmination of your expectations and the decisions you have made, based on those expectations, up to that point.

That is, you have *created your life* the way it is today by making certain decisions at different points in time that you believed would help you to achieve certain objectives. For example, you may be working as a professional because you chose to do well at school, attend university, and study hard to complete your degree; whether or not you enjoy that job is another matter. Alternatively, you may be unemployed, surviving on government benefits. Whether you currently believe me or not, this is also a result of choices you have made.

Now, sometimes you make decisions consciously but much more often you make them unconsciously. You don't even recognise them as *decisions*. You don't recognise that there is a *choice*. You do what you do because that is what you know to do and that is how you know to do it. And you know that because that is what you learned when you were a little person. This is why, even though so many people *say* that they want to be financially wealthy, so few people actually achieve it. If you didn't have anyone around you who was wealthy as you were growing up, you didn't have anyone to model, so obtaining financial wealth is going to be difficult for you.

Even though you might have a desire, you won't have a true expectation – your unconscious expectation will be what you grew up with – and your decisions will be based on your unconscious expectations. So, that is what you will achieve, unless you can find a way to change your unconscious expectation. We will be exploring how you can change your subconscious expectations later on.

## *Pause for Thought #2: How Has Your Childhood Influenced You?*

We have all been influenced by our childhoods, by the people and messages, via all kinds of media, that we were surrounded with. Take out your paper and pen again and reflect on the following.

- Who were the people around you as you were growing up and what were their attitudes to things such as money, work and education? Do you remember any particularly strong messages around any of these three things, or other issues that come to mind? (For example, "You have to work hard to make money," "No one likes their job, but you've got to do something," "You will only be respected if you get a university degree.")
- Can you see similarities between your current lifestyle and how you grew up?
    - Do you like all of these similarities, or would you like to change some of them? Which ones?
    - Why?
- Are there differences between your current lifestyle and how you grew up?
    - How did these come about?
    - Are these all positive or would you prefer to change some of them? Which ones?
    - Why?

There might be differences if you have moved to a completely different environment, for example. I grew up in a working-class family (convict ancestors and all). Members of my generation were the first, on either side of our family, to go to university. Now, generally speaking, those at university tend to be middle-class. After I graduated with my engineering degree, I worked for an engineering company for a year and a half and then moved from Adelaide to Canberra to work in a university environment. Needless to say, I had a really hard time adjusting to this new culture.

The political views of university dwellers tend to be left-wing, while I discovered that, apparently, the political views I was exposed to as I was growing up leaned slightly more to the right. (Politics wasn't really discussed around my family dinner table when I was growing up – I didn't even know what left-wing and right-wing were until I moved to Canberra!) I lost count of how many times I put my foot in my mouth. So, after many tough lessons, I changed many of my views – actually, *developed* is a more accurate description – I didn't really have many political views previously – as I said, it wasn't discussed when I was growing up. So, it is when you are immersed in a different way of thinking, either by choice or by force, that you can change your ideas about particular aspects of life. Actually, change probably isn't quite the right term here: "become educated" or "develop through exploration" are more appropriate phrases.

You can also find that a certain aspect of your life is quite different from when you grew up if the way it was as you were growing up was intolerable to you. When I was doing my PhD, I did some tutoring and laboratory demonstrating for undergraduate classes. One of the students in one of my classes also went on to do a PhD and is now a company CEO and only in his mid-thirties. Apparently, he grew up in a poor household in a situation that he found intolerable (I am not certain of the exact circumstances) and was compelled to ensure that he was never in the position of being short of money himself. I am pretty certain that his current situation does indeed ensure this.

So, it is not to say that you can't escape from your childhood influences. You absolutely can! The first and most important step is being aware. Once you are aware of what influences you had, and which ones you don't like or no longer serve you, you can start going about changing those behaviours and responses that have evolved from those influences. As the saying goes, "You are not your behaviour." Your behaviour is learned. If something can be learned, it can be unlearned – not without effort, but it is possible.

## *Emotions: Pesky or Enlightening Beacons?*

Looking back at your life so far isn't intended to be done in a harshly judgemental way. This isn't about kicking yourself for the awful things that you have done that you wish you could change, or blaming the world, your parents, your teachers, or where you grew up for things that have not turned out as you would have liked. However, it also is not meant to be void of emotion. You will need to get emotional in order to really tap into what your passions are, what's important to you, and what you really don't want to allow any more of into your life – and what you do want to allow more of!

So, why do you need to get emotional to really work out what you want in your life? Well, at our core, we all want to be happy. And happiness is, that's right, an emotion. We are emotional beings. We have feelings and, whether we realise it or not, all of our decisions are based on how we feel. Sometimes it won't be obvious why you felt the way you did and allowing yourself to explore this further can be helpful and allow you to gain insights into who you are. If you don't allow yourself to feel the emotions of your life, you will never experience the full depth and beauty of who you are and your life will never truly be yours. Unless you allow yourself to feel the emotions of past events or behaviours, you are unlikely to really get a proper understanding of why the events unfolded as they did or why you behaved as you did.

Now, by "getting emotional", I don't mean the popular and usually derogatory definition of emotional which effectively means sobbing uncontrollably for no obvious reason (although this may be appropriate at times!). I mean that you should allow yourself to acknowledge, when reflecting on the different parts of and events in your life, your feelings at those times.

There is an outdated saying in our society, that I sadly heard parroted by a young man only a year or so ago, that men are "logical" (implied as a good thing) and women are "emotional" (implied as a bad or stupid thing because it is then also assumed that they are being irrational and, therefore, coming to a "wrong" conclusion). I find this generalisation difficult to relate to as it has not been my experience. I have always seen and experienced men as being emotional as well. How could they not be? They are human, too.

I think that what the statement is actually trying to convey is the belief that women are more in touch with and more likely to act from their emotions than men are. I haven't found this to be true, either. And this is actually insulting to both men and women. Having studied and worked in male-dominated environments for close to 30 years, it has been my experience that men act and react from their emotions just as readily as women do. They just don't usually acknowledge it or, possibly, even realise it.

If you doubt this, think about a hypothetical male CEO, with a reputation for being ruthless, making the decision to make several workers redundant in order to save the company from financial ruin, rather than choosing a different option that could save their jobs. On the surface, this would seem like a logical decision because the CEO apparently made the decision based upon the logical need to keep the company in business. His argument would be that his decision was based purely and simply on the bottom line. The numbers speak for themselves. This had worked so well in the past that he gained new respect amongst his colleagues and peers and had been given a bonus for slashing costs! He had even been head-hunted, which is how he'd come to be in his current position.

So, he may not even have looked for another option, which would have saved those jobs, even if the current situation was quite different from that on previous occasions, because he had had such a positive response in the past. Why would he risk a seemingly uncertain response by doing something different when following this path had been so beneficial to him in the past? If he had tried something different he may have lost some – or all – of the respect he had gained. He may have risked his bonus, or even his job. This sounds like a very emotional decision to me.

The really unfortunate implication of the logical versus emotional sentiment, I believe, is that it is inferior to be emotional. But, humans *are* emotional. We feel. We can't help it and neither should we wish nor try to. To deny your emotions means to not allow yourself to love, to be happy, to feel elation, nor to feel sadness or disappointment. All emotions are important. They are what give life its richness and they are an indicator of what lessons are to be learned from a particular experience.

Many years ago, I developed a crush on a guy at my workplace. Initially it appeared that the feeling was mutual. In fact, it wasn't until I got some indication that he was interested in me that I had even started to think about him in that way. However, it very quickly became clear, to him at least, that we were not compatible. I was devastated for months afterwards. However, my feelings of devastation had absolutely nothing to do with him. How could they have? Nothing ever happened between us, not even a kiss. The whole episode consisted of one or two meaningful looks, some flirty emails and a dreadful night out for a drink (or several, on my part).

What I eventually came to realise, with the help of therapy, and a friend who generously gave of her time to listen to me, during what I later found out was a very stressful time for her also, was that my feelings were actually an indication of something from my childhood. I discovered that I had a deep sense of abandonment, developed from my father going away to the Vietnam War for ten months when I was two years old.

So, while my feelings were not about what I initially thought they were about, those painful emotions served an incredibly valuable purpose. They were telling me that something was very wrong in my attitude and approach to life. They served as a loud, piercing fire alarm which forced me to investigate the cause of the fire. We will explore the fire further, later in the book, and see how it is always caused by derogatory decisions you have made about yourself, usually in childhood, and have allowed yourself to continue to think and believe. So-called positive or pleasant emotions are equally indicative of constructive decisions you have made or beliefs you hold about yourself.

## Pause for Thought #3: What Are Your Emotions Telling You About You?

Taking your trusty paper and pen, it's now time to reflect on your life and how you feel about the parts of it that are important to you.

- Is there something, an issue, event or person, which you have particularly strong emotions around? These may be so-called positive emotions but this exercise is more relevant to and helpful for something that brings up so-called negative emotions.
- Write down any specific emotion or emotions that you can identify
  - That you recall you felt at the time the issue occurred or first presented itself;
  - When you think back on the issue now.
- Pick out one emotion that you have identified.
  - Identify as many situations as you can in which you feel this emotion.
  - What are the similarities between the different situations that you have identified?

We won't take this example any further for now, but what you have discovered will have opened up some doors into the way you approach life. These discoveries will be helpful in later *Pause for Thoughts*.

## Chapter 1 Review

This chapter was about starting to explore where you are and why. Armed with this knowledge, and now knowing that the beliefs and attitudes that got you here can change, you can start to make new choices. However, many of us lose our way because we get side-tracked and blindsided by all of the influences in our lives. We don't necessarily follow our dreams, if we even know what they are, because it is easier to do what is expected of us and, often, because we wouldn't know where to start to follow our dream or else we've been told we could never make any money out of them.

To make a shift, it is important to take stock of where you are and why, as you have just started to do through the *Pause for Thoughts* in this chapter, so that you know where you're starting from. As you move through this book, you'll go deeper into where you are, how you got here and where you want to go. There will be some to-ing and fro-ing on this journey as you get more and more insights both ways. As you get more insights, you'll gain more clarity and more certainty about what changes you'd like to make. Awareness is the first step to change, so once you start getting some clarity on what changes you'd like to make, you'll start to get some inkling of what to do to start making those changes.

# Chapter 2

# What Does Your Happily Ever After Look Like?

*"You don't have to be great to start, but you have to start to be great."*

ZIG ZIGLAR

We've had a look at where you are right now and how you got here. The next obvious question, then, is – where are you going? As the saying goes, if you don't know where you're going, you'll end up somewhere else! And, if you don't change anything, you'll stay exactly where you are. If you're reading this book, I am guessing that you don't like at least some things about where you are. So now would be a great time to have a closer look at those things and see what you can do to change them.

If you think about your life so far, how much of what you have in it do you feel was specifically planned and created by you, and how much of it has seemingly just "happened to you"? That's not to say that you didn't create those things that seemingly just happened to you – you definitely did – you just may not have been *aware* of yourself creating them. For example, you may be in a job that doesn't particularly excite you, or even bores you to tears. It may even involve aspects that go against your values, which lessens your motivation to put effort into it even more. Was that part of your plan for your life? When you were six, did you tell everyone, "When I grow up, I want to have a job that bores me to tears?" I am guessing not.

I suspect that what probably happened, if you are in a job that bores you to tears, is that you got caught up in the go-to-school-get-good-marks-get-a-good-job treadmill that we are all put on from the minute we are born. The problem is that this treadmill stops when you reach get-a-good-job. There aren't too many clues around about what to do, or what's possible, once you've got the good job. It's like fairy tales that end with, "And they lived happily ever after." What does happily ever after look like? And, more importantly, what would you like yours to look like?

Before we get to the nitty-gritty details of what you would like to have in your life, I'd like you to step back a bit and get a little philosophical. It has often been said that before you start detailing what you want and how you're going to get it, you need to be really clear on *why!* And that is not a simple question to answer because there are actually a number of layers to it. So, let's dive in and see what we can find out about your "why".

## Why Are You Here?

A question that humans have been grappling with, probably since we could first form a thought, is "Why am I here?" What is the point of life? There have been many suggestions of what the answer might be. An overwhelming theme, however, regardless of one's religious views, is love; the giving, receiving and experiencing of love. This can include sharing love with other people or animals. It can also include experiencing joy, which is really just an expression of love. Joy can be experienced in delighting in the beauty of nature or being immersed in the creative process, whether you're creating a painting or an elegant mathematical solution.

The tricky part can be identifying exactly what things give you joy. A good place to start is your passions, dreams and desires. What excites you? What makes you feel really alive? What inspires you? If you can answer even just one of these questions, you're on your way to really understanding why *you* are here. Don't worry if you find you can't answer any of these questions at the moment; that's what the purpose of this book is – to help you to discover the answers.

I believe that there are several layers to why you are here, or what you are here to experience. You could even call it your purpose. We've suggested that the core of why you are here is to experience love and joy. You are here to find love and joy in the people you meet, the things around you, natural and human-made, and the things that you do. Your experience of love and joy is not about the events in your life but how you choose to see those events, what you choose to learn from them and what you choose to do with what you learn.

It is easy to experience love (or joy) when you are holding a sleeping baby, playing with a puppy, or when someone gives you a long-coveted gift. It is not so easy to experience love if a waiter is rude to you, you find rubbish strewn all over your favourite, usually pristine, beach or if you are the victim of a random, violent crime. Part of experiencing love is learning to forgive. There are times you need to forgive others and there are times when you need to forgive yourself. For many of us, forgiving ourselves is harder than forgiving others, especially because we most often don't even realise that we need our own forgiveness.

Think, now, of the experiences you have had of giving and sharing. I am not talking about the unsolicited giving of advice or trying to outdo your brother in buying the most expensive birthday present for your mother. These are egocentric acts based in fear (usually of not being enough), not love. I am talking about those heart-warming experiences when you were made happy by knowing that you had made someone else happy. Maybe you rearranged an important meeting to watch your child's grand final match or stopped a complete stranger in the street to tell them that you liked their shirt. I would bet that most, if not all, of your most treasured memories involve giving and sharing – which are all about experiencing love and joy.

Actually, one time I was on an escalator and the guy behind me was wearing a great deep plum-coloured shirt. I got up the nerve to turn around and tell him that I loved his shirt and he replied, sneering at me, with "Yeah, right." I then felt a bit silly, as if I had perpetrated some dreadful social faux pas – not unheard of – and got away from him as fast as I could! Not long afterwards, it dawned on me that he probably was more used to receiving insults than compliments. (Without wishing to appear judgmental, he wasn't particularly attractive and did appear to be lacking in confidence; traits that, unfortunately, lend themselves to unpleasant treatment from others, leading him to automatically defend himself.) I hope, when it had sunk in, that he was able to feel good about my genuine compliment.

If being here to experience love and joy does not ring true for you, I suggest you stop and reflect on the question of why you think you are here for a minute or two. Let's say you come up with another reason for being here. Your reason might be that we are simply animals and our life's purpose, at its most basic level, is simply to eat, sleep and procreate. If this was true, why would we need to feel those aforementioned pesky emotions which can play such havoc with our lives? While they can be pesky, they are also what give our lives richness, the highs and lows, the euphoric moments and the desperate moments. Regardless of your answer, ask yourself if it is better than being here to experience love and joy? I really can't imagine that it could be. So let's assume from here on in, that you're coming from a base of looking for a life of love and joy.

## Spreading Love Through Your Gifts

You have been born with gifts, whether or not you have yet recognised them. As the core of your existence is to experience love and joy, part of using your gifts is to bring the experience and the understanding of love and joy to others. This is possible through sharing your gifts. This could be a tangible gift like being a talented musician, a skilled wood craftsperson or an inspirational teacher.

A gift can also be one of personality. For example, you may be blessed with a particularly happy and optimistic nature. Others can benefit both from how you react to them, being most likely in a more affirming and accepting way than others would, or from noticing and learning from how you react to others and situations that other people would react less favourably to. Notice that these are all gifts that would tend to generate good will and joyful feelings in others. (I am generally avoiding use of the words "positive" and negative" as they tend to be judgemental and do not always provide a helpful perspective.)

You can also spread love through destructive behaviours, which can also be seen as gifts. For example, if you perpetrate an act of violence on someone which causes them severe pain and trauma, they then have an opportunity to learn about forgiveness and acceptance. By experiencing such emotional and physical pain, they will have a greater appreciation of what it means to feel love and joy.

If you are a particularly pessimistic or angry person, others can also learn to experience more and greater love from these gifts of your personality or nature. If they are aware enough, this can trigger in them the recognition of an opportunity to reflect upon not only their own similar behaviours and attitudes but their reactions to yours. They can then decide to change if they feel the necessity. For example, rather than taking your anger personally and getting angry back at you, they could choose to see it as your issue (which it is) and not take it on board, not allow it to faze them. In a similar vein, many people who have experienced a potentially terminal illness, such as cancer, later say that they see having had that experience as a gift because it compelled them stop and reflect on what were really the most important things in their life. Almost without exception love is at the top of their list.

Of course, I am not suggesting that you allow your destructive emotions free-reign or just be horrible to others for the sake of it. Reasoning that anything you do to another person in such a state is okay because it's actually to their benefit because they can choose to experience more love because of it is missing the point. It's also important to recognise whether those behaviours are really serving *you* – particularly with respect to experiencing love and joy for yourself. I am simply providing you with an alternative view of the opportunities presented by the less pleasant things that can occur in your life.

Again, if the suggestion that part of your purpose in being here is to provide others with opportunities to experience more love does not ring true for you, think about your experiences with other people; even, and especially, those you really don't like or who press your buttons. For example, from those you admire, you experience joy in creating your own vision of how you would like to be, based on what you see in them. Similarly, from those you don't like, you can discover what you don't like in yourself, creating the opportunity for you to accept or change what you don't like, creating greater joy in your life. Like me, I am sure that you have people in your life who love you, people who admire you and people who don't like you so much. You are learning valuable things about yourself, and life in general, from all of these people. Does it not stand to reason, then, that others also learn from you and your gifts?

I realise that these may be quite new ideas for you. Unfortunately, in our society, we have quite an emphasis on being a victim. When something "bad" happens, it is generally seen as only an occasion for despair, anger and feeling sorry for oneself. What passes for the daily "news" is overwhelmingly about victims of crime or accidents. Many of our most popular television programs are law and order type shows with police and or lawyers helping victims by bringing criminals to "justice".

All popular programs revolve around drama. Even the so-called reality TV shows are scripted to ensure enough drama. And by "drama", I mean that so-called "problems" are introduced into the lives of one or more of the characters or participants. If, instead of seeing problems as a problem and, instead, we all saw them as just part of life and occasions of opportunity for growth and new ways of experiencing love, there would be a lot more love and joy in everyone's lives.

## Loving, Enjoying and Excelling at What You Do

So, if experiencing love and joy are the mainstays of your purpose here, then it seems logical that you should really endeavour to enjoy what you do while you are here, all of the time! In fact, nothing else makes sense! Why would you spend your time doing anything except those things that bring you joy? Really enjoying what you do has a three-fold effect.

Firstly, if you are en-*joy*-ing what you are doing, you are inherently experiencing joy. The relationship between joy and love is so close it is almost impossible to separate them. So, when you are experiencing joy you are also experiencing love. You are, then, also exuding joy and love. This naturally attracts others to you who get joy from and experience love doing the same things that you do. You then get to experience more love and joy from being with them and the experience snowballs for all of you.

Further, generally when we love what we do, we excel at it. And beholding excellence, whether it is the beauty of a sunset, the selfless kindness of a stranger or a beautifully presented meal, can be a joyous experience. I recently re-watched the YouTube video of Michael Jackson's performance of "Billie Jean" on the Motown 25th Anniversary TV special from 1983 where he did his first public moonwalk. As with all of my previous viewings of this performance (and, let's face it, practically any Michael Jackson performance), I felt absolute awe and joy at watching him. I asked myself why that was – apart from the remnants of my girlhood crush... What was it that was so special about Michael Jackson?

It finally came to me – he excelled at what he did. His performance was impeccable. Every move, every look, every "ooh!" and "aah!" was meticulously rehearsed and flawlessly executed. (The only person I know who does not experience similar feelings from watching Michael Jackson is my seven year old niece who is angry with him for taking too much medicine that wasn't good for him, which is fair enough. But that is another story.)

Another time I felt such awe that it brought me to tears was in the Uffizi Gallery in Florence, Italy. There is a painting there, by Leonardo da Vinci, which depicts a pool of water incredibly beautifully. The guide said that his teacher had been astounded at his talent even as a very young man – very few people could capture the look of water as effectively as he had done, and particularly not at such a young age. I felt quite overwhelmed by being in the presence of such talent, such achievement, by a fellow human being. It gave me an incredibly profound sense of what is possible when we discover our true talents and focus our efforts. Leonardo da Vinci clearly loved what he did – he was such a prolific creator – in both the artistic and scientific realms.

So, when we enjoy what we do, we tend to excel at it and we emanate joy and love, drawing others to us, which also opens up opportunities to teach – and learn from – them. Not only do we teach them just by being who we are – they will learn from our constructive and not quite so constructive traits – but they will also learn the experience of joy from us by being caught up in the excellence of what we do that we love and excel at.

But what is excellence? Excellence does not necessarily mean perfection. Perfection is actually an incredibly subjective term. If something is perfect, it must be perfect according to some criteria. For example, what might be a "perfect" holiday for me could result in sheer boredom for you! No, excellence in almost any area can be appreciated by anyone. Excellence is achieved through a deep understanding of the subject in which you are seeking to be excellent. It requires patience, many, many hours of study and practise, sheer hard work (though that doesn't mean to say that it is not enjoyable hard work) and a love of what you're doing and what it stands for. Excellence is about taking pride in what you are doing and caring about its execution and the results you achieve. Clearly, sloppiness is not an option!

A less obvious example of a pursuit in which excellence could be attained is that of a park ranger. If you were a park ranger, you would perform with excellence through understanding the plants and animals in your park. You would know the animals' habits, the food they eat, where they sleep, who their predators are, what diseases they can be affected by and how to recognise when they are ill.

You would know the kind of environment in which each plant thrives, what fauna (e.g., bees for flowers) they require for their health and which are to their detriment. You would understand the interactions between the different plant and animal species and know what to look for when things are not as they should be. You would know how to manage the complex set of interactions without upsetting the natural system as a whole which has, after all, evolved on its own for many thousands, if not millions, of years.

You could choose to excel at any number of things. The obvious ones are art in all its forms (singing, dancing, painting, sculpting, composing music), teaching and sports. But, what about other areas? We've just looked at the example of a park ranger, but any area or job has the potential for excellence.

If you are in a job that you feel will be difficult to get out of in a hurry, perhaps for financial reasons, why not choose to be excellent at what you are doing while you are there? For example, unfortunately, many migrants – from and in any country – and skilled or otherwise, find themselves having to start out in particularly unskilled jobs, such as cleaning. While we all know how important it is to have someone doing the cleaning (we certainly notice when it isn't done well!), there are few who would honestly wish to pursue it as a lifetime career. But, just because a job is relatively unskilled does not mean that it cannot be pursued in a spirit of excellence.

Choosing to be excellent in such a situation can have many beneficial effects. It can make you feel happier by taking pride in what you are doing and constantly looking for ways to be even better. It will make those affected by what you do happier (who doesn't like to come into a meticulously clean room – especially when someone else has cleaned it!). It could well lead to a promotion, as your excellence gets noticed by your boss, possibly making her/him more money as your work is noticed by the client and they refer the business to other clients. But, even if it doesn't, the changes it will make in your overall attitude and approach to life can only lead to better things for you in the long run.

In Viktor Frankl's *Man's Search for Meaning*, he describes the different responses of different people in the Nazi Concentration Camps of World War II. He comes very definitely to the conclusion that people have a choice in their attitude to how they see their current situation. Some of the people he was imprisoned with maintained a positive outlook despite the dreadful conditions and treatment they were subject to. Admittedly, these people were the exception rather than the rule, but it shows that, even under the vilest of circumstances, you can choose to remain positive about who you are; you do not need to let the circumstances define who you are. Pursuing excellence in whatever you do is one way of maintaining a positive expression of who you are.

*Pause for Thought #4: Where is Your Love, Joy and Excellence?*

So, one possible way of getting more love and joy into your life is to be really excellent at something. Maybe you already are but haven't recognised it yet, or haven't appreciated your gift. Grab your paper and a pen and consider the following questions, taking as long as you need to find answers that you really find compelling.

- Is there an area that you are excellent in?
    - Write it down.
    - Write down at least 10 ways you experience love and joy through being excellent in this area.
- Is there an area you would like to be excellent in?
    - Why have you chosen this area? (e.g., you've always been good at it; it looks like it'd be fun; your grandma used to do it when you were a child)
    - Write down at least 10 ways you think you would experience love and joy through being excellent in this area.
    - What do you need to do to get yourself to excellence status? Write down some concrete steps you can take to start you off.
- If nothing springs to mind that you'd like to be excellent in, can you think of a time when you experienced feelings of awe?
    - What were you doing? Were you looking at a magnificent piece of art, a stunning sunset, or an amazing electrical storm? Have you ever been moved to tears by a piece of music, marvelled at an intricate sculpture or appreciated the beauty of an elegant mathematical or engineering solution?
    - Now that you've got some creative ideas and emotions flowing more freely, go back and answer the first two questions again.
- Whatever your current situation, what can you choose to pursue excellence in today?
    - What would it mean to be excellent at that?
    - What knowledge would you have to gain?
    - What skills would you have to hone?
    - What could you change immediately (an office cleaner could leave flowers once a week, for example)?
    - What would be the benefits of pursuing excellence in this area?

## *Trauma, Forgiveness and Joy*

We have supposed that one of our main purposes in being here is to experience and understand joy and love. We talked above about different ways in which we may be able to achieve this. Here, we will explore further the implications and opportunities of experiencing a traumatic event in your life, such as suffering from an extreme act of violence.

While this is a pretty heavy topic to be talking about, especially this early in the book, it is a significant one for many people. And I believe it can be addressed in a much more constructive way than it often is in the media and society in general. If you have been affected by trauma, it could well be holding you back, stopping you from really enjoying your life. The ideas here may give you a new perspective if you have been affected by trauma yourself or through someone that you know, or even if you just find yourself despairing at what you perceive as the state of the world.

So, the question is, is it possible to experience joy after a traumatic event, or even as a result of such an event? And what is there to learn or gain from such an experience?

Recently in the news, there was a horrific story of a young woman in India who was brutally gang-raped and beaten, who died from her injuries some days later. As a result of this, the country has been galvanised to address its atrocious record of violence against women, with other horrific stories emerging, although the victims have not always died. Reading one particular story, where the victim suffered appalling internal injuries, made me feel physically ill. One of the things that was said of the victim was that she had not stopped crying in the weeks since the incident.

My heart went out to this young woman who, according to the story, was a bright student and had had a promising future ahead of her. What would her future be like now? The answer to this question is, of course, that it is completely up to her. I know that this comment could be seen as somewhat glib and lacking in empathy. However, as is so often said, by feeling sorry for ourselves and acting in ways based on that mindset, it is ourselves we are hurting, and anyone close to us. Remember Viktor Frankl's concentration camp observations (and experiences) – it is possible to choose your response, regardless of the circumstances.

Let's imagine for a second that you had a seemingly intolerable traumatic event occur in your life (I am purposely not using the term "victim"). You could choose to lament in thoughts of "Why me?" Those thoughts could be countered with "Why not you – who do you think deserved to have it happen to them instead?" A sensible response to this could, of course, be "Why did it have to happen to anyone?" But, given that it did happen, there are two possible constructive roads that I see that you could take from here.

You need to first decide that you don't know why it had to happen to anyone, but that you are not going to take it personally or as a sign that you are a bad person who deserved to be preyed upon. It may be easier to do this if you can convince yourself that no one would deserve to go through this experience. Maybe think of all of the people you know – would you truly rejoice if any of them went through what you went through; even those you aren't particularly fond of? I suspect that most of you will say "no". So, if this is true for everyone else that you know, surely it must be true for you, too. You didn't deserve it, you didn't ask for it, and it wasn't your fault.

The most constructive way that I know of to approach such an event is to look at it from the point of view of what you can learn, both in general and about yourself. Then you are free to move forward to create a fulfilling, joy-filled life, as discussed above. This is by no means a fast or an easy process, but it is an opportunity for significant personal growth. It takes time and effort, but effort that is well worth the rewards. Your life can then be unaffected by the incident in any other way, if that's what you choose. You could, for example, decide to use the incident as a stepping-stone to understand why such incidents happen at all, find ways to prevent future similar incidents, and/or help others who have been similarly traumatised to also move forward in a constructive way.

My feeling is that those who behave in such destructive ways need at least as much help as those they inflict it upon. I am not sure that our current practice of punishing people by putting them into a jail, a confined social space with others of similar destructive mindsets, is particularly helpful. How do people get to a place of such a low sense of self-worth, self-love and self-respect that they are able to carry out such horrific acts of violence against others? For the good of all, such people need our forgiveness, help and love.

I am not saying that they should just be left alone to live their lives as if nothing had happened. I don't believe that that would be at all appropriate – for them or anyone else. There certainly need to be consequences of such actions. However, I believe that more could be done to enable such people to truly rehabilitate themselves by helping them to raise their sense of self-worth, self-love and self-respect.

Sometimes, helping them and others to understand what led them to such behaviour in the first place can be helpful but this is not always necessary, nor even possible (for example, they could have been traumatized as a small child but have no memory of the incident and no one who knows about it is still alive). What we do need to have more awareness of, though, is that people act in such non-loving ways generally when they have felt unloved in some way themselves, usually over a prolonged period. This is not meant to be an excuse for such behaviour, but simply a recognition that humans are, at our core, loving beings. When we behave in ways that do not reflect this, it is generally because something has tampered with our "wiring", usually in early childhood. We will explore this idea further later.

Obviously, this is an extreme example. But what if we erased the word "victim" from our vocabularies and instead saw all experiences as simply learning or personal growth opportunities. The biggest part of our pain from having such an experience comes from what we perceive the experience says about us – that we deserved it, or that we must somehow be bad – and the fact that somewhere, perhaps very deep within us, we actually believe that this is true. That is, we tell ourselves a story about what the experience says about our own self-worth, again, as Viktor Frankl found in the concentration camps. I am not saying that it is easy to not do this as, often, the story, whether you're consciously aware of it or not, has been with you since you were very, very young. But once you are aware of this, you can start to dig up the story and then pull it apart, be free of it and live a life understanding and accepting just how worthy and lovable you really are.

### *Pause for Thought #5: How Do You Deal With Trauma?*

Learning from trauma comes from how you react to it. It's time to pick up your pen again and have a think about the following. For at least the first three questions, you will get a truer answer if you write down some examples that can back up your answer and then some examples that show the opposite. You might want to think about whether there were any extenuating circumstances for *any* of your answers and if there are any similarities in any given group of answers. For example, you might discover that you handle stress well when you've just come back from holiday (surprise, surprise!), or that you're not compassionate towards older women (maybe grandma was a rather tough, possibly bitter, character).

- Do you handle stress well? Give 2 or 3 examples of when you have handled stress well. Now, give 2 or 3 examples of when you have not handled stress well.
- How compassionate are you? Give 2 or 3 examples of when you have shown someone compassion and then some examples of when you could perhaps have shown someone compassion but didn't.

- How easily do you forgive? Are you readily able to forgive anyone for anything or do you place caveats on bestowing your forgiveness on someone who you feel has wronged you? Write down 2-3 examples each of when you have easily forgiven people and when you haven't.
- Do you often feel like you are a victim of the things that happen to you in your life? If so, step back for a second as if you were someone else observing you, particularly as you are when you feel like a victim. Ask yourself, and answer as honestly as you can:
    - What are the positive things you derive from feeling, and behaving, like a victim?

    Initially you might think that there is nothing positive that you could derive from being a victim. After all, isn't that the whole point – that something "bad" has happened to you? Give yourself some time, as much time as you need, to allow the answers to come to the surface, because there will almost certainly be some. For example, perhaps being a victim gets you more attention? Perhaps you enjoy being a victim for the drama and excitement, albeit not particularly pleasant at the time, it brings into your life? Perhaps it's actually allowing you to hide from yourself how lonely or insignificant you feel. Perhaps you're afraid that if you weren't filling your life with being a victim, there wouldn't be anything else to fill it with.
- Have you experienced a traumatic event in your life?
    - If so, how did you react to it? Why do you think you reacted in this way? (You might want to take into account your answers to the previous questions when thinking about your answer to this one.)
    - Have you been able to accept and move forward, or have you allowed yourself to hang on to destructive feelings and thoughts around the incident? Why do you think this is?
- The following question may be a bit confronting and require some really careful thinking – particularly if you still have quite a strong emotional charge around the experience.
    - Write down all of the benefits having had this traumatic event occur has brought into your life. For example, it may have brought you more loving attention from family and friends, allowing you to be the centre of attention more than ever before (maybe you rarely or never were before); it may have been so physically injurious that you have been declared unfit for work, which has forced you to find other interests for which you've discovered a real passion; it may have compelled you to start or contribute (your time, money, skills,

experience) to a foundation for other people affected by a similar trauma or even a completely different cause, which has benefitted many people and gives you great personal satisfaction; you may have met some amazingly compassionate caring people who are now great friends, who you would not otherwise have come into contact with; you may have become more compassionate yourself and now like yourself better.

- When you've completed the previous question, consider your answers.
  - Were there some surprises, some positive things that you hadn't considered previously?
  - Were there some things that you had previously always considered to be negative but discovered a positive spin to them?

If you haven't experienced a traumatic event in your life, it is still worthwhile considering how you generally react to even relatively minor stressful situations. For example, if a shop assistant is rude to you, do you stew about it for the rest of the day, or do you assume that they've just had a bad day and don't give it another thought once you've left the shop? If you hand in a draft report to your boss and it comes back with lots of corrections, how do you respond? Do you immediately get defensive and not look at it for days because you can't handle the perceived personal criticism, or do you go and get a cup of tea so that you can sit down in a relaxed fashion to read their comments and consider why they have made the points they have made and if they will truly improve the report? It may be that you realise that if you had looked through it again in a week, you would have made the same suggested changes yourself.

You will have the opportunity for plenty more self-reflection throughout this book and you may find that the same themes keep recurring. For example, you may find that the theme of needing to be the centre of attention keeps coming up – perhaps from a feeling of being ignored, or invisible, as a child – or you might find that you have a strong need to be right. I became aware, just a few years ago, that I had a strong need to "do the right thing."

One way this manifested itself was that I used to get very annoyed with people who pressed (or, more accurately, bashed) the pedestrian button at traffic lights, especially if they did it several times out of impatience. I realised I was being silly, but I used to get a rush of angry frustration every time I saw this happen, because, having studied engineering and computer science, I knew that the button just needed to be pressed once to register that a pedestrian was there. Pressing the button several times doesn't make the lights change more quickly (except, sometimes, very late at night and very early in the morning). So, bashing the hell out of it doesn't make any difference, except that it could break it!

When I realised where my feelings were coming from, I was able to calm down about it. (And, besides, they make the buttons much more robust these days because, apparently, people just love to bash buttons...) I still get a twinge, but I don't get as stressed as I used to now that I'm aware of where the rush of feelings comes from – I can separate them from what is currently happening. This situation sounds silly, and trivial, but that is how insidious these things can be – until you have an awareness of what your reactions are about, it can be very difficult to mitigate them, let alone eradicate them!

For now, just look back at your answers for *Pause for Thought #5* and see if there are any behaviours or reactions that have provided you with an "Aha!" moment, a new perspective, that you think you could change or incorporate immediately. Often, just having the "Aha!" can be enough to largely eradicate, or at least mitigate, an old behaviour or response.

## *Chapter 2 Review*

To uncover what your happily ever after life ideally looks like, you need to have a grasp on what you believe life is about; what does a purposeful life look like for you in general terms, at least? We have suggested here that it must revolve around, or at least include, copious amounts of love and joy. One way of achieving this is through the pursuit of excellence in some endeavour. We have also looked at the opportunities in learning from others and at your role in teaching others through your constructive and destructive behaviours.

In order to find an effective way forward for yourself, you also need to understand how you react to certain things, particularly stressful situations (anyone can be well-behaved when they're happy and life is easy!). If you can understand yourself in this way, you may then be able to change your behaviour, by changing your attitude, if you wish. Putting all of these things together gives you a solid foundation for moving forward, on your way to a fulfilling, joyous life.

# Chapter 3

# Creating a Fulfilling and Meaningful Life

*"Strive not to be a person of success, but rather a person of value."*

ALBERT EINSTEIN

The first step towards changing your life for the better is awareness of what you'd like to change. Change will not happen if you have no awareness that change is necessary or even possible. Once you have awareness that change may be a useful thing in your life, the next step is to determine *what* needs to change and, finally, *how* you might be able to make it happen.

If you're reading this book, the chances are that you're not feeling completely fulfilled in your life. That is, you at least have a sense that things are not quite how you'd like them to be, even if you haven't identified what things. For that to change, something in your life needs to change. In this chapter, we're going to look at what needs have to be met for you to feel completely fulfilled. We're not talking at a physical level, here, but at a mental or psychological level.

You'll have the opportunity to discover which of these needs are driving you (there can be more than one) – that is, how you approach your job, other people and just daily life. Then you'll be able to see how this may or may not be serving you. If you decide that being driven by these needs is not serving you at this point in your life, this is an excellent place to look for change. Changing which needs you are driven by can alter your whole outlook on life, which can change what kinds of people and situations you attract to you, as well as what opportunities you take notice of – and bring you closer to living a fulfilling, meaningful life. So, let's dive in!

## The Six Human Needs

A quick search on the web will uncover a number of descriptions of the basic human needs, which differ depending upon the focus. Some are very detailed with respect to your physical needs and others are more focussed on your psychological well-being. The version that I have found the most useful was developed by Anthony Robbins. Anthony Robbins is one of the foremost success coaches in the world today, having worked with U.S. Presidents and world-class sports people. I highly recommend that you check him out if you haven't previously come across him.

Being aware of these needs will help you to understand why you continue to do certain things even if you logically know that they're not constructive or beneficial to you. I will introduce Anthony's six human needs first and then talk about how they impact on you as a whole and how you can use them to change your habits and your life.

The first human need is that of CERTAINTY. You must have a minimum level of certainty in your life to feel comfortable. The minimum is different for everyone. Certainty is tied in with feeling safe and secure, from having a roof over your head and having enough food to eat to feeling safe from being physically attacked. This need is why you watch your favourite movie over and over again – you know what happens and how it is going to make you feel.

It is why you yearn for your own bed when you have been travelling away from home a little too long. It is why you go to the same place to get your coffee every day and why you got married (or perhaps why you didn't!). It is why, when you are feeling a bit down, you put on that old jumper which everyone else tells you is a bit scruffy, but for you it's soft, warm, and comforting. It is why, even though you never eat McDonalds at home, you do when you're in a foreign country and have had enough of trying to guess the menu items in local restaurants. And, sadly, it is also why people stay in jobs that they hate or stay in abusive relationships. In a twisted kind of way, as unpleasant as these situations are, they are comfortable – you know what to expect.

The next human need is that of variety, or UNCERTAINTY. While you must have a minimum level of certainty in your life, if you have too much, you get bored! Again, the level is different for everyone. Your need for uncertainty is why you might be attracted to extreme sports like white-water rafting, base jumping or canyon tight-rope walking (without a net!). Your need for uncertainty is why you might love horror movies. You might like to travel on a regular basis to new places or try a different restaurant every month or even every week. You might take up a new hobby each year or change jobs every few years, either through promotion or through changing companies. On an everyday level, it's why you don't wear the same clothes every day or cook the same meal every night.

The next human need is the need for SIGNIFICANCE. You need to feel important in some way; a bit special. Significance can also be obtained through being a bit different from others, having some trait, skill or talent that makes you stand out from the crowd. A feeling of significance can also be gained in the moment through a spontaneous, "crazy" action – this is often referred to as showing off! There are many ways in which to feel significant. You might have gained a feeling of significance by obtaining several letters after your name through study. You can feel significant by wearing slightly different clothes to the norm, by having tattoos, body piercings or colouring your hair bright blue.

Often you don't even have to achieve a significant goal to feel significant, you just have to tell people that you are aiming for that goal. How impressed would people be if you told them you were training for the Olympics? You don't even have to make the team to have some effect. You might feel significant by always having the latest trends – in anything – fashion or technology, or always being the first to see the new release blockbuster movies.

Some people gain their feelings of significance by being notorious. How significant would Australian bushranger Ned Kelly feel if he were alive today? And you can bet those people who choose to make a statement to the world by going out and shooting up a school or becoming a suicide bomber feel pretty damned significant, too. So, a feeling of significance is often tied up with something that you choose to identify yourself with such as a distinguishing physical feature (manufactured or natural), an activity that you undertake, or your job.

The fourth human need is that of feeling LOVE AND CONNECTION. Love is about giving and receiving. This need requires little explanation, but it is why we all seek a mate. Or you will hear of people finding love through their children when their intimate relationship isn't giving them the connection they need. Many people also get this need at least partly fulfilled through having pets. And, of course, we can have great friends with whom we share a close connection, and whom we love. We can feel a sense of connection through exchanging a smile or a greeting with a stranger we pass on the street.

The fifth human need is that of PERSONAL GROWTH. You need to feel that you are growing as a person, expanding your outlook and ideas. You need to be exposed to new ideas and experiences that make you think deeply about the world you live in – physical, cultural and spiritual, and question what you previously believed to be true. Imagine if you just believed everything you learned as a child and stopped taking in new ideas at the age of twelve. The world would be a very scary place if it was run by a bunch of people who were effectively twelve years old (although I am sure we all wonder if this is not true at times).

In fact, this is why our world leaders tend to be over the age of fifty. Indeed, anyone who becomes a president or prime minister at an age below that is termed "young" - just about the only time someone in their forties is labelled that way. This is because, in addition to natural biological maturity, people who have lived longer have generally had more experiences and been exposed to more ideas, and had time to more fully digest and evaluate them. That is, they have learned and grown. While this is, of course, not a true reflection of the comparison between every person and every other person younger than them, it is generally true of those in a position to vie for a presidency or prime ministership. But even if you aspire to a less ambitious station in life, you still have an inherent need for growth.

The sixth and final human need is that of CONTRIBUTION. You need to feel that you have something to contribute to your fellow human beings and that you are actually doing so, that you are making a difference. This is why you might do volunteer work whether it be to visit people in old folks' homes, work at an animal shelter, or plant trees when your local council calls for help. You might choose a job that clearly fits into this category, like teaching or being a park ranger.

You may have noticed that many of the examples could have been used to illustrate more than one of the needs. For example, in being a volunteer, rather than being driven by the need to make a *contribution*, you could wish to be seen as a good person in the eyes of your neighbours, a form of one-upmanship, perhaps, so it could also have been used for the need of *significance*. If you volunteer at an animal shelter, you may also be meeting your need for *love and connection* through working with animals. Going to get your coffee from the same place every day could also fulfil your need for *connection* if you have been going there long enough that the staff know you and you have a good rapport with them.

If you are into extreme sports, not only is this meeting your need for *variety* but it is almost certainly meeting your need for *significance*. They're not called "extreme" sports for nothing – most people won't go near them, so that makes you just that little bit cooler than the average person; or a lot cooler depending on how extreme your extreme sport of choice is. In fact, if anything that you do meets at least three of these six human needs, it becomes a habit or even an addiction. This can be a constructive influence in our lives, or it can be destructive. Whether it is constructive or destructive depends on which combination of needs is involved and what it is that you're doing to meet these needs.

## What Are Your Predominant Needs?

You will tend to have one or two needs from which perspective you tend to approach most things in your life. For most people in Western societies, these are the needs of *significance* and *certainty*, in one order or the other. This is largely because of the way our society is structured. It is greatly based on the need for certainty (you've got to get a good job so you'll be able to pay the bills) and significance (work hard so you can climb the corporate ladder). If you've been applying the above examples to yourself, and been honest with yourself, you are likely to already have a pretty good idea of which needs you are driven by the most.

To properly determine which needs you are driven by most of the time, consider the activities you spend most of your time doing in a typical week or month. You might also include those activities that are generally not so frequent, such as going on vacation. While the nature of the activities themselves is a clue to the needs you are most trying to meet, it isn't the whole story, as we got a hint of in the examples above.

What also counts is your attitude to those activities and your underlying reason or reasons for pursuing them. For example, you might go on vacation every three months – lucky you! – which would imply the need for *variety* as a driver. However, if you go to the same place every time, that would also imply the need for *certainty* as a driver. If you go to a much coveted and glamorous destination such as Rome or Monte Carlo, you may also be meeting your need for *significance* – "Oh, yes, we're off to Monte Carlo again. The hotel where we usually stay has set aside our usual room." So, in this example you have at least three of your needs being met. No wonder you keep going back so often – it's become a habit!

Actually, when I was in my twenties, I was planning for my first trip to Europe with my then boyfriend. We were going to go on one of those "twenty countries in three days" tours. My boss at the time was very well travelled and travelled often. One place he did know well was Paris, and he very kindly wanted to tell me about the best places to go – where to shop and what was a must see, and so on. During our conversation he very matter-of-factly made a comment along the lines of, "…where I usually stay in Paris…" I don't mean to imply that he was showing off – he was the kind of person who just really enjoyed life and took that kind of thing in his stride.

This comment really caught my imagination and I decided that one day I wanted to be able to say that too! As luck would have it, I have been fortunate enough to visit Paris several times in the years since, both for work and on vacation, and I am rather pleased to say that I can now say that. And, yes, I admit I definitely get my need for significance partially met in being able to say that!

In *Pause for Thought #5*, you looked at whether you ever feel like you're a victim because of things that have happened in your life. You explored the positive things that may come to you from feeling and behaving like a victim. If you did the exercise properly, it is almost certain that you did come up with a couple of positive things, or even several, which resulted from you behaving as a victim. You may now be able to see how these fit in with meeting some of your six human needs.

For example, acting the victim may give you more attention from others, which could fulfil your need for love and connection. This could also meet your need for significance, through the attention itself and you may use being a victim as your identity. Giving ourselves an identity is nearly always tied up with the need for significance. You might also find that being a victim can meet some of your other needs as well. With these new insights, you may want to go back and try that exercise again.

Another example might be if you are a member of an activist group that does things like holds rallies and prepares and presents petitions for politicians or other controlling or overseeing bodies. The initial assumption might be that you are doing this to make a *contribution*, which is almost certainly true, particularly if it is something particularly emotive that you strongly believe in like gay marriage or the right of women to choose to have abortions. However, there are other needs that you could also be meeting.

Particularly if you are one of the leaders of the group, or aspire to be, you might be meeting your need for *significance*. Just having a cause to fight for is a very common way of meeting the need for significance. If your group is constantly coming up with new ways of pushing for your cause, then your need for *variety* is likely being met, also. If it is a particularly emotive cause and, let's face it, most of them are, then you are likely to be feeling, if not love, then certainly *connection* with the others in your group, as you have a sense of belonging and common purpose. That's four needs already!

You could also be experiencing *growth* as you do more and more research on your cause and find yourself questioning why you really believe what you do about it, trying to understand the points of view of your opponents and whether it is worth continuing the fight. That's five. If you stay with the group for a reasonable period of time, so that you are very comfortable there and have a good handle on how things work, you would probably also be meeting your need for *certainty*. That's all six!

The most telling thing, then, is which needs are really *driving* your participation in an activity. If you jump from cause to cause, it is likely that your need for *variety* or *significance* is driving your participation – as you don't care what the cause is, you just like the adrenalin rush of being part of this kind of group. If your brother is gay and has had a hard time of it, and you want to do something to show him support and so become active in the gay marriage movement, *love and connection* might be your driving force. Or if you are a physically challenged lawyer, you may see an opportunity to use your skills and meet your need to make a *contribution* to the cause of improved amenities for people with similar challenges.

While all six needs are vital, we have already discussed the idea that the main reason you are here is to experience love and joy. So, to experience love and joy, it is from the place of the latter three needs, love and connection, personal growth and contribution, that you want to be approaching most of what you do, particularly love and connection. You will still need to be meeting the first three, but they should more often be met *as a consequence* of what you do, rather than as the drivers for what you do, or at least be a secondary driver to one or more of the latter three.

## Pause for Thought #6: Working Out Your Main Needs Drivers

To help you understand the kinds of things that might indicate being driven by a particular need and to help work out which needs you are currently mostly driven by, you might like to try the following exercises. They are a somewhat tongue-in-cheek look at what someone might be like if they were driven by each of the six human needs in two different scenarios: in the workplace and outside the workplace. You might find that you are driven by more than one.

### Your Needs Drivers At Work

**Certainty:** You've been in the same position for quite some time and you're content there for now. Your job has certain set tasks that need to be carried out on a regular basis, at least every week, if not every day. You try to avoid dealing too much with people.

**Variety:** If someone asked you to describe a typical day in your job, you wouldn't be able to do it. Every day brings something new and it's just so exciting! And you wouldn't have it any other way. Although, you do complain a lot about how you can never get through your emails. Some people describe you as bubbly. Others don't.

**Significance:** Your eye is on the corner office. You have a job that is seen as prestigious like a lawyer or doctor. Or else you're the managing director or CEO of your company – or aiming to be. You might have several degrees or even a PhD. You're constantly looking for the next promotion. And you're likely to get it.

**Love and Connection:** Your job involves a lot of contact with people, a lot of talking where you are able to be a bit chatty and maybe get a bit personal. This is the part you love most about your job. It might be something in retail, sales, tourism or hospitality, for example, where you can provide some service to the people you deal with and you love being able to help in this way.

**Personal Growth:** You do all of the professional development courses that are offered. You particularly like the ones that offer you the chance to learn more about dealing with people – the so-called "soft" skills. The

"Significance" people think that you just like getting out of doing "real" work.

**Contribution:** You hate to see suffering and, as part of your job, you are able to alleviate it in some way, usually so that a number of people, preferably many, can benefit, not just one or two. You often bake cakes to bring in to share at the office.

## Your Needs Drivers in Your Extra-Curricular Activities

**Certainty:** Once a month, you and your partner go to the same restaurant for your date night. You've been going there for as long as you can remember. It's your favourite place in your city. Not that you've been to many others. But you know what to expect and you usually order the same thing; although sometimes you order the sticky date pudding for dessert instead of the tiramisu.

**Variety:** You start a new hobby every 3-6 months. You look forward to the Adult Education magazine landing in your mailbox so you can decide what course to do next. You have lots of unfinished projects around the house. Your spouse complains about them.

**Significance:** You go to high-brow events such as art exhibitions, the opera and the ballet. You don't necessarily know a lot about them but it is very important that you're seen there. You also brunch at a trendy cafe every Sunday. If you've got kids, you're on the P&C committee – as the president.

**Love and Connection:** You spend most of your leisure time with your family, either your kids or your extended family. You may even have one or two foster children.

**Personal Growth:** You do meditation or yoga, or both. You have several audios and videos by people like Anthony Robbins, or Deepak Chopra. You have at least one book by or about the Dalai Lama. If you haven't already, one day you plan to make a homage to an ashram.

**Contribution:** You volunteer. A lot. You are passionate about the organisations that you volunteer for, and they are most likely to involve helping children, animals, or those disadvantaged in some way. You probably sponsor two or more children through a charity.

You would have recognised aspects of yourself in the above examples. If you didn't, you may need time to let the six human needs idea evolve in your head for a while. If this idea is quite new to you, it can be difficult to see past what you have always assumed was normal or natural. It may not have occurred to you that there could be any other way of thinking or of approaching things – at least not for you.

I recall one workshop participant who came up to me to tell me that she hadn't recognised herself at all in any of the descriptions. She went on to say that she was quite bored with life and had no real energy or enthusiasm for anything. This, to me, said that she was driven very strongly by the need for certainty. If she was bored and yet had no enthusiasm to try anything new or do anything different, she was clearly not willing to step outside her comfort zone.

## Exploring Your Needs Drivers Through Your Patterns

Another way of working out your needs drivers is to explore the patterns that you have in your life. They are a very strong indicator of what is driving you. We all have patterns that recur in our lives, whether or not we are aware of them. Usually it is easier to see the patterns in other people's lives than in our own.

You may know someone who is constantly getting into relationships with the same type of partner who is clearly (to everyone else) wrong for them. This is possibly an indication of a *certainty* driver – perhaps these partners have a behaviour that is the same as that of one of their parents, so at least they know what to expect from such a person even if it's not always pleasant. Or maybe you know someone who always seems to receive bad service – no matter whether it's at a restaurant or a mechanic – and they always put in a complaint about it, which they get nowhere with. This is an indication of having *significance* as a driver. Sometimes our patterns are more positive, like the person who always not only gets good service but gets a bonus as well, like extra chocolates with their coffee from a friendly waiter. (I know someone like this. I was constantly in awe of what I saw him get away with. At least he was kind enough to share the free chocolates with me.)

## *Pause for Thought #7: Your Patterns*

Regardless of whether you're aware of your own patterns, you have them. Take out your paper and pen and ponder over the following questions. Be as honest and open with yourself as you can. Once you have finished each one, reflect on what needs drivers you think any patterns you have identified may indicate. You may wish to read back over the examples given earlier in the chapter for some clues.

- Think back over the intimate relationships that you've had. Write down as many similarities as you can between all of them. To make this easier, you might want to make a column for each relationship (or perhaps just the most significant ones) and list all of the traits you can recall either of the person themselves or the relationship. Then compare the columns to see what patterns emerge. Perhaps writing a trait for one relationship or ex-partner may trigger a realisation that it also existed in another.
- Repeat the previous exercise, but this time consider your friends, rather than your intimate relationships.
- Now consider the jobs you have had. You may wish to consider the culture, your relationships with your colleagues, location, tasks, and level of responsibility you've had for each.
- Finally, look back at the hobbies you've had over your life.

If you're feeling brave and you have a friend or close relative that you trust and feel safe with, you might want to ask them to answer the above questions for you, too. Perhaps you could do an exchange and do it for each other – that way, you're both putting yourselves on the line! If they are the right person to ask, they will tell you from a place of love and not from a sense of spite, malice, or judgement. If you're feeling really brave, you might want to try it with a few different people and look for the commonalities or, indeed, patterns in what they tell you. That way you can separate one person's projections of their own stuff from what might actually be true about you.

If several people are making the same observations about you, those observations might be worth exploring further. If you do choose to do this, though, a word of caution; you need to be ready, open-minded and trust that those you have asked are coming from a place of love. If this is your intent when you approach them to do this for you, they are more likely to actually approach it in this way. It is quite possible that you will hear things that may be hard or confronting for you to hear. What you need to remember is that you only have to take on what is true for you. However, make sure you are being honest with yourself; otherwise it is only yourself that you are deceiving, and the exercise will have been a waste of time for everyone.

## *Where Do Your Patterns Come From?*

While many of our patterns come about as a consequence of behaviours we learnt from our parents, or through our circumstances as we were growing up, and can be fairly easy to recognise, others may be less obvious. It can be the case that some of your patterns, and the strong underlying emotions attached to these, developed from a much earlier, childhood event that was never appropriately addressed or dealt with. Often this is because it happened at a time before you could speak or else you were not able to express how you felt either through lack of vocabulary, or else because no one thought to ask or listen.

While the idea that our early childhood experiences have a profound effect on us throughout our lives is becoming more widely known, the full implications of it are still not generally well understood. I have several times heard or read of people expressing the idea that young children won't remember what happens to them when they're young, so it doesn't matter so much if they get upset by something. This is, unfortunately, far from the truth.

While young children may not remember things in the way that adults do because they don't have the words to express how they're feeling, those feelings will remain in their memories. And they will be all the more intense because emotions are all they have to express themselves with. They will always be there somewhere under the surface and they may never work out why or where they came from. There will just be an underlying sense of something awry, that they may not even be aware of because of its familiarity, that will affect the way they approach everything for the rest of their lives.

I remember reading an interview with a woman whose husband was in jail overseas. She said that she had told her children that Daddy wouldn't come home unless they were good. I was horrified! What an awful thing to do to lead those children to believe, not only that it was their fault if their father didn't come home, but that it was because they were bad. I realise that the mother was probably highly stressed in this situation. It would not have been easy for her caring for her children on her own and not knowing when her husband was going to come home, if ever. But, unfortunately, such a thoughtless comment, especially if it was often repeated, could possibly have had quite a profound effect on her children's self-esteem for the rest of their lives.

I believe that this is why many people have what society refers to as a mid-life crisis. I believe that it largely stems from unresolved childhood trauma. In my own case, when my father went to the Vietnam War, he didn't go once, but twice. That is, he went away when I was two and a half, he came back some months later, stayed for two weeks for a break, and then he left again for several more months. As a three year old, a few days' separation from a parent is a long time, let alone a few months. And there is just no explanation that is going to convince a three year old that "Daddy has to go away." This gave me the sense throughout my childhood that my dad could just up and leave at any moment. However, I did not become aware of this sense until I was nearly thirty years old. It came out as a sudden revelation during a conversation I had with a friend.

Who knows what effect this had on my childhood and early adulthood, the decisions I made and actions I took, or did not take. One can imagine that this did not provide me with a strong sense of security during my childhood. I do not wish to overstate the seriousness of this situation as, compared to what many people go through, this was relatively mild. I was, at least, safe with and loved by my mother during the time that my father was away. However, it does give you an understanding of the kinds of effects that emotionally destructive events, such as the deprivation of a parent for a period of time, can have on a small child.

## *Chapter 3 Review*

There are six basic human needs which we all strive to fulfil in one way or another, often several ways at once. What can make a big difference to our lives, to how happy we are, and how fulfilled we feel overall, is which of these needs we choose to use as our drivers and which we leave to be met consequentially. While we can be driven by different needs in different parts of our lives, such as work versus home, most of us have just one or two needs that drive our behaviour the majority of the time. In our culture (and just about any modern culture) these two needs for most people are certainty and significance. Choosing to be driven, instead, by love and connection, personal growth or making a contribution can give us a whole new perspective of the possibilities that life has to offer and turn our lives completely around.

# Chapter 4

# Escaping the Human Zoo

*"If the misery of the poor be caused not by the laws of nature but by our institutions, great is our sin."*

CHARLES DARWIN

Have you ever been to a zoo? If, like me, you've been going for some time (since the 1970s, say) you will have noticed a large change in the structure and presentation of zoos. The enclosures (we don't call them cages anymore) tend to be a lot greener, with a lot less concrete. They are getting closer and closer to emulating each animal's natural habitat. This is great news because why would an animal that is used to living in a jungle or on a great, expansive plain want to live in a concrete box?

But what is still missing is the animal's opportunity to hunt and forage for its own food, mix naturally with its own kind (often animals, through scarcity, are kept on their own in the zoo) and travel any distance, as it might do in the wild. Each animal species has evolved to survive and thrive in *its natural environment*. Part of survival must include good mental health as well as physical health. So it makes sense, then, that if any part of any animal's natural behaviour is stifled, its well-being is likely to suffer.

The offspring of any animals in the zoo won't know any different. They won't consciously miss their natural habitat. However, they will, like their parents, yearn for it because they have been wired, over many millennia, to thrive in their natural habitat. That doesn't mean they wouldn't or couldn't thrive in other habitats, it's just that zoos aren't usually such a place.

And so it is with humans. In almost all ways, the way we live is not in our natural habitat – so we effectively live in a zoo. We live in man-made enclosures, although, admittedly, we can generally come and go as we please within our zoo – and our environment does tend to involve a lot of concrete. We eat food that someone else has hunted and gathered for us. We rarely spend time in nature, if we even know where – or what – it is. The biggest problem with this is simply that it doesn't occur to most of us that we are living in a zoo and that that might be a part of why we don't yet feel that we've found our ideal life. Once we do realise this, then we can do something about it.

The great thing about being a human is that we have free will and are incredibly resourceful. Once you become aware that you're actually living in a zoo, and that part of the reason that you're not feeling fulfilled is because you're not honouring the way you evolved as well as you could be, you can start doing something about it. If you look hard enough, you'll find the key to let you out of not only your enclosure, but out of the zoo. You'll be able to create the habitat that suits you best and enables you to truly thrive.

*Getting Back to Basics*

You almost certainly know that humans evolved as hunter-gatherers. We had no permanent homes in the sense that we now have them. We moved with the seasons and the food. We would have very much thought of ourselves as part of the environment and would have naturally evolved to extract the best out of the plants and animals that existed there with us, without exploiting them unnecessarily to their, or our own, detriment. A reasonable part of our days would have consisted of hunting, gathering and preparing food. This would have been a communal activity that would have included everyone in the community, young and old, so there was no separation of work, family and community.

These societies were often egalitarian in that men and women shared the hunting and gathering duties and there was no concept of hierarchy because material possessions were a burden to carry from place to place. Everyone would have had a place and a role. Everyone would have felt useful – that they were making a contribution – and that they were loved and belonged. There was no need to climb the corporate ladder to be deemed a success (or significant) because there was no concept of success. Everyone was fulfilled just by being a part of and contributing to the community.

When there wasn't food to be gathered, hunted, or prepared, their time would have been spent teaching, learning and playing. The older people would have taught the younger people about hunting, gathering and preparing food; understanding nature and how to find or create shelter. And this would have been fun for all involved, because so many of the six human needs would have been met for both the older ones doing the teaching and the younger ones doing the learning.

The older ones would have felt significant for having knowledge to share and the younger ones for being taught that knowledge. There would have been a lot of love in the community as any jealousies and resentments would have to have been dealt with swiftly and effectively, otherwise they could have led to the demise of the tribe. It was, therefore, in everyone's interests to love and care for everyone else.

The older ones would have felt that they were making a contribution by teaching the younger ones and the younger ones would have had their need for growth met through learning new things – that would then lead to them being able to make a contribution. Everyone's needs for certainty would have been met through this tight-knit community living and they would have had their need for variety met at the very least through teaching and learning different tasks and moving with the seasons and the food. For the little ones there would have been a lot of play and discovery. You only need to watch a small child for a few seconds to know that not only are we innately curious creatures, but we also naturally want to play and have fun. Many of us lose that by the time we are adults; just introducing more fun into our lives could have a transforming effect on many of us.

The need to be in a natural environment fending for oneself is, sadly, seen in the neurotic or depressed behaviour of animals kept in zoos, who are denied this pleasure. This is particularly prominent in enclosures in which there is neither the room nor the opportunity to express innate behaviours, evolved for survival and, consequently, mental and physical health. Such behaviours include not only hunting and gathering food, but also moving from place to place with the seasons. Imagine if you had to stay in your house ALL the time, never even going to the corner shop. You would go stir-crazy!

Our need for food and our need for knowledge of how to protect ourselves from predators would have cultivated our curiosity in learning the minute details of our surroundings, as evidenced by the excellent tracking skills of people in existing tribal communities. By observing our environment so carefully, we would also have developed an intimate understanding of what flora, fauna, weather and habitat types affected each other. In this way, we would have learned how to take actions that were not detrimental to other parts of the environment, at least as far as they affected our own survival.

This is what the Australian Aborigines mean when they talk about "belonging to the land". A nice example of this is the way they used to catch fish. They would form a catching pool in the river, using rocks, ensuring that they were positioned so that only the bigger, more mature fish were caught and the smaller, younger ones could continue on their way. This ensured future breeding and an ongoing supply of fish.

Somehow, though, we seem to have lost a lot of these basic skills which would have brought us much pleasure. Apart from a few pockets of people still living in traditional tribal ways, modern society is all about convenience. Many of us have lost our connection with the land, our natural environment, and with it, our appreciation of the intricacies and beauty of a less materialistic way of life. The fact of animals in zoos being depressed due to not being able to express their natural behaviours, applies equally well to humans. Our world is so structured and restrictive in many ways, it is akin to being in a zoo and so it is no wonder that mental health is such an issue, particularly in western societies. The obesity epidemic is almost certainly one consequence of this as many of us indulge in "emotional eating" to numb our pain. So, how does this separation from nature and our natural tendencies affect you and what can you do about it?

### Have We Gone Off-Balance?

Over the past decade or so, the term "work-life balance" has increasingly cropped up in the popular media and popular psychology articles. That term, "work-life balance", has always bothered me. Who decided that "work" is not a part of "life"? Maybe it is just sloppy terminology. Maybe "work-play balance" is what they really mean. But then I would have to ask – who decided that work could not be play? I think that what is actually meant is "work-family-community balance". And the reason that this is currently an issue is because of the structure we have developed in our society. We have separated "work" from family. We have separated family from community. And we have separated community from work.

I recall many years ago when I had just started at a new job, in a new city where I knew no one, one of my colleagues announced at morning tea that she didn't make friends with people at work. I suspect it was directed at me, as I was the only new person there in need of friends and perhaps she felt this was a good way to let me know she didn't want to be friends with me without being too direct or obvious. Regardless of her actual intent, I found it an odd and sad thing to say. Given that we spend most of our waking hours in our workplace, why wouldn't you want to be friends with the people you meet there? However, I know she is not alone in this sentiment.

We did not evolve in an environment that required us to put on a uniform or a suit, travel in the monotony of peak-hour traffic or a train carriage for countless hours, then sit behind a desk for eight hours before making the return journey home, five days a week. In fact, we didn't evolve in an environment in which a "week" even existed. All of these constructs are wholly human-made. It is not that being human-made is, in and of itself, bad; but we do need to carefully consider the efficacy of any human-made construct, whether physical or conceptual.

We all know that many things in modern life, human-made things, are harmful - though we don't always admit it – either to humans, the natural environment (land, water, air) or animals and their habitats. We tend to forget that, as humans, we are animals and a part of the environment. Indeed, for centuries man has seen the environment, including animals, as something to be conquered and controlled. This is understandable to a certain degree as we naturally look to make the most of what is available to us.

However, it has rather gotten out of hand. The world's environmental system is incredibly complex. It has evolved over millions and millions of years. It has developed as a set of intricate relationships that are essential to the well-being of the whole – the whole that provides food, water and shelter for our survival. So any changes or interventions we choose to make need to be very carefully considered, researched and planned.

Human intervention has had disastrous consequences time and time again. An example is the introduction of the cane toad to eliminate the cane beetle which was destroying sugar cane crops in Queensland. With no native predators, the cane toad is now a huge pest and is gradually spreading its way across the continent – seemingly indestructible – except, perhaps, by the odd vehicle wheel. And, apparently, they failed at reducing the numbers of cane beetles at all. It's a bit like the old lady who swallowed a fly – her chosen remedies were, ultimately, futile.

Of course humans have also created many, many things which have made all of our lives easier, more comfortable, and more convenient. My intent, here, is simply to point out that not all "progress" is good. To live truly happy lives we need to be a bit choosy about what kinds of "progress" we accept into our individual and collective lives and where we would be much better off sticking to traditional or more basic ways of doing things – for the sake of our mental and physical health, and that of our planet.

For example, I love convenience as much as anyone. Driving to work so that I can have an extra 15 minutes of sleep is often very appealing. However, walking for 20 minutes to get there, instead, is much better for me as it clears my mind before I get there, and it gets my body moving, which sets me up for the day in a much more healthy way. How many things are you doing in your life because they are convenient, comfortable or you just haven't thought about them, that could be swapped for a simpler, back-to-basics alternative that is more beneficial to you overall?

*Satisfying Your Inner Hunter-Gatherer*

In our modern world of amassing material possessions, where does one stop? If you do get to be the richest person in the world with the most houses, the biggest swimming pool, the most designer clothes, shoes and jewels, helicopters, private jets and sports cars, then what? What will having all of those material possessions do for you? What will it mean? What will you aim for next? Will you just be striving to maintain your number one position? Although, how will you know? And, even if you do know, maybe at least in terms of overall wealth or assets, how will you maintain it? What if you can't maintain it – will you have failed? What will that mean? Now, obviously, this is all getting a bit silly, but I hope it has started you thinking about what you are aiming for in your life and why.

Obviously, we can't go back to the hunter-gatherer days. For a start, most of us don't know how to hunt and wouldn't have a clue what to gather! If we look at the basic characteristics of the hunter-gatherer lifestyle, they included collecting our own food, teamwork, community, play and a sense of being part of nature rather than separate from it. I believe that to truly follow your passion, you would be starting from a much more solid base if you were to pare back your life, remove what is really not necessary and introduce more of the basic pleasures, like spending more time in nature and perhaps even growing some of your own food.

Satisfying those core hunter-gatherer characteristics can be relatively simple. Let's start with collecting your own food. The obvious starting point is growing your own fruit and vegetables, or even just start with some herbs in pots on your kitchen windowsill. If you're already doing some or all of these things, maybe think about getting some chickens for their eggs. If you live in a flat or an apartment with no garden, plenty of cities and towns have places for community gardens. Getting involved in one of these may even fit in better with the hunter-gatherer way.

If you really can't face gardening – maybe you have a brown thumb like me – maybe just being as basic as possible with the foods that you do bring into your home will suffice. I love the feeling of coming home with my groceries and having a full fridge and pantry. It is a mixture of excitement at the yummy meals to come, and the satisfaction of knowing that they will also be good for me – a dash of self-righteousness, perhaps. I guess this satisfies the gatherer in me. This feeling only really occurs when I buy fresh produce – fruit, vegetables, nuts and meat. I rarely buy junk food or much in the way of processed foods but, when I do, the feeling is more of guilty pleasure, which is nowhere near as nice and certainly not satisfying.

I believe that this is also why "retail therapy" is so popular. There is definitely a bit of hunting and gathering going on. In fact, when I go shopping and I am looking for a particular type of item, say a cream jumper (which I am definitely a sucker for), and I find one that I like in the first or second shop that I look in, it isn't nearly as satisfying as when I have to look in four or five shops before I find the perfect jumper.

In fact, even if I don't find what I'm looking for, there is a certain sense of satisfaction in having just had the chance to forage for it! And maybe this is also part of the reason why we fairly quickly become tired of such items – hunting and gathering were for food which tended to be eaten that day, requiring a new excursion the following day for more food. This constant need for something new probably also developed to make sure that we chose different types of foods over a period of time to provide our bodies with a diverse enough variety of nutrients.

*Pause for Thought #8: Your Inner Hunter-Gatherer*

It's time for you to reflect on your own life and what can be pared back and simplified and what you can do more of to help you to satisfy your inner hunter-gatherer. Take your paper and pen and, for each of the areas of: collecting food, teamwork, community, play and being part of nature, answer the following questions.

- Write down all of the ways in which this area is satisfied in your life right now.
- Could any of these ways be improved upon? Can you include your family more? Or would it be better if they were removed altogether (the ways, not your family!)?
- Could any new ways be introduced?
- Ideally, and if you haven't thought of any so far, can you approach this characteristic in ways that don't require any money, or that are less expensive than what you are spending on them now?

Now that you've considered each of the characteristics separately:

- Are there any things or activities that you can do that combine two or more of the characteristics? For example, if you go berry picking, you are combining being in nature with gathering food.

How do you feel, now, looking at some of your answers to the above? Excited? Is there perhaps even a sense of relief? If so, where do you think that might come from? Spend some time now, with your family if you have one, and make a plan to introduce at least one new thing, or new way of doing something, into your routine every couple of weeks for as long as it takes to introduce all of the ideas you've come up with. I know your life, and level of happiness, will be transformed within months, if not weeks.

*Physical-Spiritual Being - Your Inner Rulebook*

We've talked about changing your physical world in ways that satisfy your inner hunter-gatherer to transform the amount of happiness, love and joy in your life. But what about the world inside you? Taking notice and care of this is paramount to living a happy and fulfilling life. There is no reason why it shouldn't be possible for you to experience love and joy constantly. That is not to say that it is easy, but I would bet that if you are reading this, it is almost certainly possible to experience them more often and under a wider range of circumstances than you currently do. The key to this is satisfying both your physical being and your spiritual being.

Whether or not you believe in a spirit that survives physical death, you can still be spiritual and have spirituality in your life; some of the most spiritual people I know believe that death is the end of their existence. It is about tuning in to your physical-spiritual being and living according to what you hear.

We have all heard the saying "You can't take it with you when you die". Of course this means that when you die, all of your material possessions remain behind for your relatives to squabble over. Similarly, when you arrived, you did not bring any material possessions with you. (Indeed, it is every parent's lament that babies come with no instruction manual!)

Unfortunately, too, you arrived without a rulebook or a guidebook, not even a page of hints for how to be an effective human being. As a child, then, you relied on those around you for clues on everything from how you should behave, to what you should eat and what attire is acceptable. We talked earlier about how children are born copycats and look to the bigger people around them for how to survive. And it has always been this way.

I read somewhere recently that what you are willing to eat as an adult largely depends on what you grew up eating. What people in some countries consider a delicacy, people brought up in other countries wouldn't put to their lips for all the money in the world. Indeed, I have a friend from India who won't eat runny egg-yolks – which I think are really yummy – particularly when eaten with toast soldiers! I, on the other hand will probably never be convinced to eat monkeys' brains! Why should this be?

Regardless of whether you believe in evolution or creationism, and give or take a genetic deviation or two, we all have the same tastebuds and the same stomachs. If eating something doesn't make someone else sick, it won't make you sick either, unless you tell yourself it will (food allergies notwithstanding).

People who live in the same region not only eat the same things but they speak the same language – with the same accent – and wear the same kinds of clothes. For example, regardless of wealth, women all over India wear saris. They may be more or less lavish in the richness of their cloth, and the amount of sparkly, spangly bits, but they are still generally worn across the country. Women in Australia, as a general rule, do not; unless they were originally from India or somewhere in that region.

I have always found it interesting that people born in a country with a distinctive style of dress continue to wear that dress on a daily basis even when they have lived in another country, with a completely different style of dress, for many years. Perhaps you have noticed this, or experienced it, yourself. They stand out like a sore thumb, as the saying goes, marking themselves immediately as a "foreigner".

Sometimes this can bring favourable attention, but we also know that it can bring very unfavourable attention from those who feel threatened by anything different. So why would they do it? The most logical explanation is that the comfort provided by wearing such a familiar garment, with such close links to home, is overwhelmingly stronger than any discomfort experienced by a few thoughtless taunts. Obviously racial tensions are a lot more complicated than this but you get my point.

In a similar vein, people who live in the same region tend to have the same religious or spiritual beliefs. Again, this comes about through being influenced, as a child, by the big people around you. Children will tend to take on the beliefs of their parents, particularly when this provides them with a strong sense of belonging. Few people enjoy being singled out as different, unless it is in a particularly positive way, like being singled out for a much admired talent such as a great singing voice. Such a "difference" is likely to make you more popular. Choosing to go against a cultural norm, though, such as with religious beliefs, can result in ostracism and even, in extreme cases, death.

Generally, then, much of how you live your life, including your beliefs, values and even preferences in music, appears to be very much dependent on where (and when) you grew up. That is, it is determined by factors *outside* of you. If, as we explored earlier, the main purpose of your life is about experiencing joy and love, and if you agree that we are all physically essentially the same and, therefore, mentally and emotionally the same at our core, then maybe all of this outside stuff is really just ornamental and doesn't really matter so much?

### *What if You Didn't Get the Memo About the Bible?*

I believe that we are spiritual beings who are here to experience a physical existence before journeying back into the spiritual world, though I do not consider myself as belonging to any particular organised religion. My feeling is that many people find organised religion useful in terms of providing meaningful guidance on how to conduct their lives. Certainly, the authoritative books for the world's main religions, such as the Christian Bible, contain a wealth of wisdom and spiritually enlightening understanding. By living your life by truly following the basic messages championed in the Bible, and the other great religious books, I believe that you would live what would generally be considered as a "good" life.

I want you to imagine our early ancestors who existed prior to the development of writing and even prior to the development of language. Perhaps you are imagining "cavewomen" and "cavemen" when we were hunter-gatherers. Not only were they also not born with rulebooks, but the big people at that time didn't have rulebooks (or a Bible) either because writing hadn't been invented yet. So, while they may have developed understandings and practices around basic survival issues such as getting food, finding shelter and finding a mate, I am pretty sure they wouldn't have had any creeds around which days of the week they were allowed to eat certain foods, for instance. For a start, they would have had no concept of days of the week.

I would also bet that a big part of their existence was having fun and being joyful. Just think of any animal and, particularly, baby animals. Except, perhaps, for the more primitive creatures, such as insects, you can easily see the love between any mother and her babies. Love is just about the only constant amongst all animals and, indeed, amongst all humans. If you take everything else away, all of the dogma, the rituals, the cultural behaviours, everything that is different between humans in different regions, the one thing that you will find in common, apart from the need for the basics for physical survival, is love. And everyone can smile. And laugh.

The point I am making with all of this is that finding "the truth" about life and what your purpose is here and how you're meant to go about it is a very tricky business. The best you can do then is to determine the truth as it is for you. The obvious next question, then, is how do you do that? The most sensible answer, it seems to me, is to search within yourself. Perhaps you actually were born with a rulebook, but it is inside of you. Maybe only you can truly know what is the best decision or approach for you in what are often complex circumstances.

Reading widely, travelling, getting involved in your community and taking in a broad range of ideas – really experiencing life – is certainly worth doing. At the very least it will help you to understand the decisions and approaches of others. At best it will help you to hone and clarify your own ideas. You will notice in your exploring that, while there are differences in the detail, there are some common themes that show up consistently, such as the values of forgiveness, love and kindness. While exploring the ideas of others from throughout the ages has great merit, and goodness knows there has been a lot of wisdom recorded over the centuries, your own inner-wisdom is the best rulebook for you to follow. Meditation is one of the best ways I know of tuning in to it.

## *Meditation - Tuning In To Your Internal Rulebook*

Meditation effectively calms your mind and allows you to sit in the stillness. When you do this, not allowing yourself to be distracted by things outside of yourself, it gives your mind the space to go beneath all of the surface stuff that is largely the result of what you get fed through daily life. Underneath, you'll find real wisdom that is directly of benefit to you. It is the place you'll find the gold nuggets that are left for you after your subconscious has filtered out the guff that's not relevant or of interest to you. These nuggets are what make up your inner rule book. If everyone on Earth meditated for just 15 minutes per day, the world would be a much calmer, more loving place to be.

I had my first introduction to meditation when I was in my mid-twenties. I remember that the teacher would lower the lights, have some candles burning and play some ethereal-sounding, relaxing music. It was really nice. However, I also recall feeling that I wasn't really getting into it, at least not initially. I recall being distracted by tickling feelings on my cheeks or a stray fringe hair brushing my forehead. I think I was initially expecting too much – not that I really knew what to expect. I think I was hoping to have visions of heavenly beings bringing me joyous messages of how they were watching over me and how loved I was and that everything was fine just the way it was. While this wasn't quite the way it turned out, I did start having more definite meditation experiences – generally a feeling of deep relaxation and letting go – rather than just closing my eyes and having my mind wander, fairly quickly.

There are many different meditation techniques that you can try. You may find that you prefer one over all others, or you may change your preference depending on your mood or state of mind. The simplest technique is just to focus on your breathing. You don't need any special equipment, nor do you need to sit cross-legged in the lotus position. The main thing is that you are seated comfortably. Some people even meditate lying down. I have found this to be less successful for me, as I tend to fall asleep!

Regardless of what technique I am trying, except for yoga, I find that my meditations are most effective when I am sitting up as straight as possible, possibly, but not necessarily, leaning against something (a wall or a chair back).

The point of focussing on the breath is simply to give your mind something to focus on so that it is not simply wandering. You can meditate with your eyes open but, when you are first learning, it is probably best to keep your eyes closed to minimise the opportunities for distraction.

So, sitting up straight and comfortable with your eyes closed, and your mouth closed, breathe in and out through your nose. Your focus should be on whatever seems most natural to you. It could be on the opening of the nostrils where the air is entering and leaving your body, the area of skin between the nose and the mouth or on the movement of your diaphragm, in and out, as you breathe. It doesn't really matter, as long as it is consistent. Breathe at a comfortable pace, as slow as you like, and definitely not too quickly. Your mind will wander. That's okay. When you realise that it is wandering, let those thoughts float away and just bring your focus back to your breathing.

One of the reasons breathing is chosen as a focus is because it is something you have control over and it is generally rhythmic which helps you to relax into the meditation. A similar effect can be accomplished with your eyes open by focussing on a candle or a picture. The more you practice, the more energised you will find you feel after your meditation sessions. I find that I feel less focussed and less calm on the days that I don't begin with meditation, like something is missing.

There are many different sensations you can experience during a really good meditation session. You can feel like your whole body is buzzing and energized. You can feel almost like you're floating, lifting up into the air, free of your body. As you become more practiced, you can also try noticing the gaps at the end of each in-breath and each out-breath. There is a small gap at the end of breathing in, just before you breathe out and at the end of breathing out, just before you breathe in. The gap is almost like a stopping in time, a nothingness. As you become aware of this gap you can attempt to expand it by making it last a little longer. Once you are practiced at this, and obviously there are practical limits to how long you can make it, you can then practice extending the feeling in the gap through the next breath to the next gap. In this gap you will truly experience no thought. It feels incredibly calming.

There are other, external tools you can use for meditation. Many people listen to audio recordings of various kinds to help their focus during meditation. Two kinds that I have found particularly helpful are binaural beats and guided meditations. There are hundreds of both of these available. Binaural beats are created by playing one single-frequency tone in one ear and another tone, close in frequency, but not quite the same, in the other ear. You can't actually hear the binaural beats, themselves, as they are hidden under a soundtrack of some kind, such as music or falling rain. The brain "hears" the very low sound frequency that is the difference between the two binaural frequencies, which helps to slow it down and allows you to more easily go into a meditative state.

Guided meditations usually have music playing in the background, although this isn't necessary, with someone speaking over the music guiding your thoughts. The meditation may be on a particular topic such as overcoming your issues around money or your health, or it may be simply about relaxing the different parts of your body, or relaxing by imagining a walk through a beautiful forest. I find that guided meditations work best for me when I am having trouble calming my thoughts by myself, such as when I am finding the things that are happening in my life to be unusually stressful.

Other times, I find that guided meditations, and those with just the music, are counter-productive to my meditation. For example, the music or guidance might change in a way that isn't where I want to go at that point, so it can feel a little jarring. However, this can be a matter of experimentation. Once you have listened to a particular guided or music meditation a few times you will know what to expect and your meditation will be smooth.

I certainly find that my mind is much clearer and I am much calmer when I keep to a regular meditation routine. My life is more "in the flow". I find that ideas and inspiration come to me more easily and life is less confusing. Meditation is seen as a way of communicating with your greater wisdom held in your subconscious mind. By shutting out the noise of the rest of the world, you allow messages from your inner knowing to float up into your conscious mind for direct use, making for wiser decisions and a more self-assured ride through life's gauntlet.

## Chapter 4 Review

Humans have travelled a long way from how we evolved. In many ways this has been beneficial for us and, in others, it has been less so. The important thing is to remember that we have evolved over time and that some changes may not be the best for us in terms of our mental and physical health and for just being happy. In order to live a truly passionate life, you need to get back to your physical and spiritual roots. Taking stock of where you currently are and simplifying to get some way back to your hunter-gatherer roots can provide you with a strong base to spring from.

Being more aware of the things that you have in your life that may not be enhancing your happiness is a great start to weeding such things out and setting you on the path to a much freer, happier life. Sometimes just tweaking a few things in your life, like taking a walk in nature once a week, can be all it takes to make some quite major mindset shifts.

In addition to reacquainting yourself with your dormant hunter-gatherer, taking some time every day to look inside yourself and listen to your own inner wisdom can greatly improve your inner sense of peace and happiness. You can make great strides in as little as 15 minutes a day. Remember, you are here to experience love and joy. Finding them can be remarkably simple.

# Chapter 5

# What's Possible?

*"Why, sometimes I've believed as many as six impossible things before breakfast."*

LEWIS CARROLL

This book is about creating a wonderful life, the most wonderful life imaginable to you. There is nothing like embodying the feeling of unadulterated freedom that comes from the realisation that you really are here to live the life that *you* want to live. Not the life that your parents want you to live. Not the life that you think your friends expect you to live. And possibly not even the life your spouse thinks you should live. The tricky part is truly embracing what this means.

Before we get into the real nitty-gritty of identifying exactly what you are passionate about, we are going to have a look at some of the reasons why we hold ourselves back, or pretend that we can't think of anything that we really want to do. We are very adept at sabotaging ourselves without realising that is what we are doing. Then we are going to look at a few common passions and the enormous variety of different ways each of these passions can be expressed in our lives. You will almost certainly be able to come up with plenty of your own ideas and variations as well. By giving you a sample of what's possible in a few areas that people are commonly passionate about, it should be easier for you to home in on what you are passionate about, and how you would like to approach it, when we get to exploring your passion in the next chapter.

While you are reading this chapter, I want you to pretend you could be anybody you wanted to be. You don't have to picture who they are – they just don't have to be you. Imagine you're starting with a clean slate. And then let your imagination go crazy. Imagine that anything is possible. If it's easier for you, pretend you're reading this chapter for someone else. We tend to be able to solve others' "problems" much more readily than our own, so if that works for you in this chapter, by all means, try it.

## What is Really Going to Make You Happy?

When we think of following our passion, most of us envisage that our passion will make us not only extraordinarily happy, but extraordinarily wealthy as well! And there is definitely nothing wrong with that. In fact, I insist that you start thinking that following your passion – whether you've identified it yet, or not – will bring you both great happiness and great material wealth. Once you start thinking this way, it gets working on your subconscious which starts looking for ways to make it happen (we'll talk about your subconscious in more detail later).

When we imagine a life of wealth for ourselves, we usually immediately think of the fabled life of a movie star, rolling in money, with flashy cars, private jets and enormous mansions on every continent around the world. However, this lifestyle, or the financial wealth required to live it, seems too far out of reach to most people. They can't see how to start let alone how they can possibly get there, so they never actually get started. Further, many people find this kind of lifestyle less than tasteful – maybe because of the tabloid stories we hear of a few celebrities, or the biases of the messages of our childhoods (how often did you hear phrases like "Filthy rich", "We can't afford that", or even "You can't be spiritual *and* rich"?).

One of the problems I see is that we rarely hear about the lives of people who are both financially wealthy and truly happy, *that we can relate to*. The ones we hear about tend to be larger than life such as, for example, Sir Richard Branson. And that's the point – the ones we *hear* about. What about the ones we don't hear about? There are thousands, if not millions, of seemingly ordinary wealthy people living fun, joy-filled lives who we never get to hear about.

They go about doing what they love to do without shouting about it to the world. They can do it without ceremony and without creating controversy. We hear about the problems celebrities have with the paparazzi, but this does not apply to all celebrities. Many of them we only hear about when they want us to, like when they have a new movie to promote, or wish to raise awareness of some cause close to their hearts, although, unfortunately, they usually get more media coverage for the movie.

So, we need to get past the idea that living an abundant, passionate life has to include aspects like celebrity or being larger than life, unless being a celebrity naturally appeals to you or you are naturally larger than life. That is the key. You don't have to be anything but you. This doesn't mean that you won't have to step outside your comfort zone once in a while. In fact, if you're not stepping outside your comfort zone on a regular basis, you're not growing. And, if you're not growing, the saying goes, you're dying.

Most of us have a reasonable idea of what things in life naturally appeal to us – even if we have, until now, been unable or too afraid to explore them. In uncovering and living your ideal life, you're searching for more of who you are. You don't have to know everything you want at the beginning of the journey of your wonderful life. You'll discover new ideas and possibilities along the way. So it will be a constantly evolving existence. Reading this book and doing the reflections will help you to identify at least one or two "must haves" for what would make an ideal life for you that will enable you to move forward with more clarity and sense of purpose along your path.

While it is absolutely not necessary to have a belief in a God or an afterlife, in order to create a life full of abundance, wealth, health, love and joy, it has been my experience that those who have the most success with the principles discussed in this book do have at least some sense of a spiritual part of themselves, in one form or another. That is, they have a sense that they are a part of something greater than themselves and that they are here to contribute to that. In other words, they have a belief that they are here to make the world a better place *because they are in it*.

## Overcoming Underlying Resistance

So, now to the question that I asked in the chapter title: What's Possible? What's possible is *whatever you can imagine*. Now, that's a pretty big statement and I know that some of you recoiled at it, didn't you? Or your stomach muscles might have tightened. That recoiling or stomach tightening is due to *resistance*. If you are experiencing resistance, that is perfectly okay, and perfectly normal. It is just your subconscious telling you, through physical means – your body – that it is scared, that you are pushing at the boundaries of what it is comfortable with. The concept you have encountered is counter to what it has learned is the best way to keep you safe and, therefore, how it has allowed you to operate up until now. (We'll talk more about how your subconscious works for you, later in the book.)

Feeling resistance like this is also an opportunity to learn the lesson behind that resistance and break yourself free from its hold over you. You probably have running through your mind questions like: but don't I have to work at least 100 hours a week to be really successful?; but I'm 80 and I want to be an astronaut; but what will my friends and family say? Let's look at these questions one at a time, because they each have different core beliefs attached to them and different ways for us to unravel them.

## Doesn't Being Successful Take a LOT of Hard Work?

The first question was: "But don't I have to work at least 100 hours a week to be really successful?" The basic underlying belief for this question is that you have to work hard to be successful. The second unspoken underlying belief for this question is that working hard is *painful* or *undesirable*. And it is this second belief, in particular, that stops us from succeeding. Generally speaking, people who are successful at a particular thing do work hard to be successful at it. However, when it is something that they are truly passionate about, they don't notice that they are working hard because they love what they are doing! In fact, it is almost like an addiction – they can't help themselves but work at it whenever possible because they love it so much.

For example, while it is perhaps not the most constructive of activities, children (and many adults) can spend hours playing an interactive computer game (if they're allowed to!) but complain about having to spend two minutes doing something as simple as cleaning their teeth. They are passionate about the computer game. They are so immersed in it that time ceases to exist for them. Most computer games require a reasonable amount of skill and many also require determining and using strategies and tactics, knowledge of which can only be acquired through practice, or *work*. So, the key, then, is to make sure you are doing something constructive that you also find really fun and stimulating.

Remember the six human needs, being, certainty, variety, significance, love and connection, personal growth, and contribution? If any activity we undertake does not meet at least one of these needs, we are unlikely to spend long doing it. Ideally what you spend your time doing will encompass meeting at least two of love and connection, growth or contribution.

Doing something that you are passionate about will also meet your need for certainty. This could be certainty in knowing how you will feel when you do it, whether that is a sense of purpose, a sense of comfort from doing something that you know or just being happy doing something that you love. You could also feel certainty in your confidence in your skills in the area of your passion. When you have worked hard, or practised, enough, you will get to a point where you are really good or even excellent at your chosen activity. This will almost certainly meet your need for feeling significant. In this instance it will be a nice side-effect rather than your driving force.

## How Do I Want to Feel?

The second resistance question was: "But I'm 80 and I want to be an astronaut." I admit that this one *seems* unattainable. Initially it seems almost akin to saying "I want to be the Queen of England." For most of us, it has an exceedingly low probability of physically happening. So, what to do with such improbable imaginings? I am a strong believer in the idea of true belief enabling us to achieve anything that we want to achieve, no matter how impossible it may initially seem, as long as we know what it really is that we hope to get from achieving it and have actually chosen our achievement target appropriately.

The reality is that some of our apparent desires will initially seem to come under the banner of "ridiculous". The task, then, is to determine what is actually at the core of the desire for that experience.

The desire for any experience is always associated with how that experience will make you *feel*. So you need to determine what it is that you want to feel. This then opens up new, potentially more attainable, possibilities for you to consider. So, in this particular example, perhaps the underlying desire is simply to do something really thrilling and somewhat outrageous. Perhaps you could replace it with sky-diving (maybe in a tuxedo or ball gown, or dressed as your favourite Simpsons character).

Another possibility is that you may be able to slightly broaden your desire. For example, an 80 year old is unlikely to be accepted into any official space program, as an astronaut but, with commercial space travel on the verge of attainment, actually travelling into space at any age and level of physical well-being is approaching possibility. You just need to find the money to pay for it.

## What Will My Family Think?

The third resistance question was: "But what will my friends and family say"? If you find yourself asking this question then you really need to break it down to find the core issue. This kind of question is often related to fear of not "belonging" to the group that you most identify yourself with. We will talk later about your friends and when it might be time to let a friendship go. Your family, of course, is a different issue. As they say, you can choose your friends but you can't choose your family. So, how do you deal with the possibility of being rejected by your family if you choose to do something out of your family's norm?

A really enlightening exercise is to write down all of the positives about your relationships with your family members (or those you are particularly concerned about), as they currently are. Then write down all of the negatives. There are no rights or wrongs, this is all about your perception. Try to come up with as many negatives as you did positives. (I am assuming that if you were concerned about losing or jeopardising your relationship with certain family members, then you perceived that there are currently more positives than negatives.)

Now repeat the exercise from the perspective of how you think it might be if you pursue your dream. You may find that it isn't likely to be as bad as you thought and that, in fact, there are as many positives as there are negatives. (Dr. John Demartini provides a great argument for there being equal amounts of positive and negative in any situation; that everything is in perfect balance or equilibrium.)

If you find that you think the negatives will outweigh the positives, then this is a pretty clear indication that, in your current mindset (which is neither good or bad – it just is), you will be unlikely to be able to achieve your dream as your subconscious will be focussing on the negatives and wanting to protect you from them. (We'll talk more about how your subconscious affects you in a later chapter.) So, what to do with your dream? This will depend on a number of factors, including exactly what the negatives are and exactly what the positives are. Maybe you haven't found compelling enough positives yet. To remedy this, you may need to develop your dream a little, or a lot, to make it more compelling for you.

For example, say your dream is to open a hairdressing salon but everyone in your family has been a lawyer for the past three generations. You fear that you will be frowned upon for not being ambitious enough, or you won't be able to earn enough money to keep up with lawyers' pay packets. One possibility is that you could make your dream quite ambitious by focussing on a high-end beauty salon which offers high quality massages, make-up, nails, facials, hair treatments and hairdressing, using all organic beauty products (maybe from your own label), providing you with a higher level of prestige – and income.

However, it may be that you never really liked the stuffiness of all that law-talk anyway, nor all of the pressure they always seemed to be under, including the long hours and the keeping up of appearances. Maybe it is your wish to have a simpler life and hairdressing is something you've always liked the idea of and, actually, you have a bit of a flair for it. So, it might be that you think they will look down on you and you're not sure that you can handle that. If this is the case, there are two main options.

Either, you decide that having a hairdressing salon is a true expression of who you are and that, if you approach it from that place and it makes you happy, they will see that and accept it too, even if it means some discomfort for a year or two while they adjust and you establish yourself. Or, if you don't think you can overcome your fear of being looked down upon, even if hairdressing is a true expression of who you are, then you may need to look at which of the six human needs are driving you in your pursuit of this dream.

Maybe you wanted to pursue it to prove a point (fulfilling your need for significance by being the black sheep in the family) rather than coming from a place of true joy. On the other hand, if you believe that your driving need or needs are love and connection, growth and/or contribution, perhaps you can massage your dream in some way that will lessen the negatives. Take a look at the negatives in your second list from the above exercise, and see if they give you any clues as to how you could change your dream in a way that still satisfies your desires, but lessens these potential negative impacts.

## *The Fear Factor*

Then of course there are many other questions which fall into the category of "excuse" as a result of fear. The fear is either of success or failure. Really, the best way to tackle this is to just get stuck in. As I said above, you just need to take a step, take some action. You don't need to know how it will all unfold, you just need to do something constructive that will take you closer to doing something that you think you'd love to do – even if your vision changes later. Write down some thoughts, make a phone call, or set up a meeting.

For example, if your dream is to write a book, you could take the following actions:

- Write down some thoughts on content.
- Write down some potential titles.
- Engage an authorship coach to guide you through it – and keep you accountable!
- Write down some chapter outlines.
- Choose a few articles for research and read them.
- Schedule time in your calendar every day to write, whether it is fifteen minutes or two hours.

If your dream is to start a business, your actions could include:

- Register a business name.
- Make an appointment with an accountant.
- Determine your budget and what you can do with it.
- Register a domain name for your webpage.
- Set up a business Facebook page.
- Define your target market - who do you want your business to serve?
- Find some short courses on running a business and enrol in them.

See how simple this is? You don't have to take great leaps to make progress. You just need to consistently take small steps. If you have identified your passion, I'll bet you can think of at least half a dozen things you could do, right this second, to start making your dream a reality. We'll go through some of the common steps later in the book, but the ideas here should at least whet your appetite and get you realising how simple getting started actually is.

*Ferreting Out Resistance*

As the above examples illustrate, when people say that they want to change but never quite seem to get around to doing it, or claim that they are content, or that they see no reason to change or improve themselves, this often really means that they are quite fearful inside. It is your natural state to be curious, to be joyful, and to be growing. (If you don't believe me, spend some time with a two-year old child! They haven't been too tainted by society's expectations, yet, and naturally allow their true selves to shine through.)

People who refuse to seek growth are generally afraid of either what they might lose if they change something, what they might gain or what they might find out about themselves, or others; what they might have to face that has been buried for years, maybe even decades. This fear is completely understandable. However, that doesn't mean it can't be overcome. In practically every case, facing the fear is rarely as bad as we think it's going to be, and the rewards once we make it through to the other side can be breathtaking.

## Sunita's Story

Sunita had been saying for at least three years that she wanted to start a business based on her passion for designing women's sportswear, but somehow she never got beyond looking up potential website names. When she finally accepted that she was holding herself back for some reason, and did some reflection exercises, she came to the realisation that she hadn't progressed any further because she was afraid that her husband would not understand her need to change, wouldn't like it, and would leave her. The perceived security she experienced from being in a relationship with him outweighed her desire for following her passion, given her current perspective of what was important in her life, which, of course, explained how she had got to this point in the first place – you get what you focus on.

Being aware of what was holding her back was the first step to moving forward, because then she could start to dismantle her fears and find ways of addressing them. Of course, she may have been right about her husband and that is where his fears come in to muddy the waters. He could well have felt threatened by her courage and what other changes this might have led to her making and what those changes meant for him. Part of his feelings of being threatened could have been from a sense of not being in control, particularly when he first heard of Sunita's desire for change and, even more particularly, if she had been clearly on the brink of making changes that he wasn't ready for. A further complication could have occurred around the meanings he placed on her need for change.

Because of his own internal issues, her husband may have subconsciously interpreted her need for change as a rejection of him. Like Sunita, he may have been unaware, consciously, of why he reacted in the way that he did. Until they were both aware of the nature of their reactions and behaviours – that is, as a consequence of fear – it would have been difficult, if not impossible, for them to sort through and address them. Without doing this, the most likely outcome would have been that Sunita would never have made the change, but then would have sunk further and further into feelings of lack of fulfilment, possibly eventually forcing a change anyway, by deciding to leave her partner, assuming that he was the cause of her unhappiness.

If they did both become aware of what was causing their reactions, it is possible that they could have decided to split after all, realising that they didn't want the same things, or they could have found ways to address their fears and moved through it together. Either way, at least they would have been making their decisions consciously.

Particularly from Sunita's point of view, this is an example of fear of loss. She was afraid of losing her partner and the perceived security having a partner gave her. And, when we get right down to it, that is what most of our fears are around – security (and fulfilling that need for certainty). So, in order to make the changes that you've started envisaging for yourself from the ideas and exercises in this book, you'll need to convince yourself that it will be worthwhile going to the effort that you will need to go to.

You will need to convince yourself that your new way of being, first and foremost will provide you with at least as strong a sense of security as your current situation does. And if you can't convince yourself of that, then at least one of your other six basic human needs is going to be fulfilled in a really big way in order to make up for the shortfall.

## *A World of Possibilities for Your Passion*

Okay, so you've recognised and overcome your resistance and excuses. You may even know what your passion is (don't worry if you don't, we're going to delve into that in the next chapter). But, what is possible? We're going to look at some basic ideas which can apply to just about any passion and then flesh out these ideas for a few specific passion examples.

With just about any area that you might be passionate about, there are some common basics that you can start with to get some ideas going. And you don't have to choose just one approach for your passion, you can have a whole raft; although, you might like to start with one and build from there. So, let's get stuck in.

Figure 2: Basic framework for creating a way to live your passion

You can be a *teacher* or a *creator*. Perhaps you can start teaching to give you an income stream while you build up your creator role (e.g. piano teacher versus keyboard player in a band, or composer). You could consider a closely allied role which utilises other skills and passions such as writing and travel. Thus, options such as being a historian, professional critic, biographer or themed tour organiser are possibilities. These could be narrowed down by choosing a particular genre or specialty. Then there is the question of whether you want to work for yourself or be an employee. These elements are shown in Figure 2.

So, to tailor this framework for your particular passion, you would start with the basic framework and then add details which are relevant to your passion. We'll look at some examples, now, to give you the idea.

## The Consummate Foodie

Let's say you're a passionate foodie. Actually, just calling yourself a "foodie" says to the world that you're passionate about food – and not just any food, but really good food! However, food is a pretty broad area. There are so many aspects to food and not all of them will necessarily appeal to you. For example, do you like growing, cooking or just eating food? So, let's start with the main ideas – those in circles – in Figure 2.

How could you be involved with food as a creator? You could be a chef who creates your own recipes in a Michelin-starred restaurant, or a cook in a cosy café who makes others' recipes. Then you'd need to determine a specialty. And there are so many yummy areas to choose from with food; my mouth's watering just thinking about them! Would you like to focus on pastries, cakes, desserts, chocolate, lollies, main meals, vegetarian/vegan, health food, or a particular cultural theme, such as Indian, Mexican or Mediterranean?

Do you want to work in a restaurant, or café, or from home? Do you want to be the employer where maybe you own the restaurant but aren't particularly interested in cooking the food yourself, you just like the whole show around presenting and eating food; or would you prefer to be an employee so that you can focus on the food itself, rather than the business? Maybe you'd be happy to run a franchise that already has everything set up for you and you can just run with their ideas – particularly if their ideas and values align with your own. Do you want flexibility in your hours or a set routine? There is also the option of doing catering; perhaps even being an in-home chef for special occasions. You could do this from home as a one-person operation and build it up over time – if you wanted to.

Perhaps you see yourself sharing your knowledge of food with others through teaching. You could just run short courses in your area of particular interest as part of an informal adult education program or else work for a cooking school of some description. If you're not sure of your particular area of interest, you could try running a number of different short courses to see which you like best. You could do this without even leaving your current job. It would be low cost in both money and time. If you're really ambitious, you could start your own school!

Maybe you don't want to actually cook at all – at least not as the main part of what you do. Maybe you are interested in writing about food, perhaps from a cultural or historical point of view. This could involve travel, too. Or perhaps you love both travel and food, and would enjoy organising specialist tours that revolve around food. You could do tours to particular regions or countries to savour individual cuisines, or visit several different places for contrasting cuisines.

You could go further out still and consider nutrition as an area related to food. Again, you could go through the whole range of possible modalities. An extra one for this is one-on-one clients; although, as a cook in the teaching genre, you could also take on one-on-one clients.

Other aspects you could consider include whether you have a passion for fresh food or if you're okay with pre-prepared – the pre-prepared meal market is really booming, with everyone getting busier and busier. Perhaps you like the idea of gourmet hampers for corporations. What kind of theme suits you best – fun, colourful, sophisticated, homely or a combination? Then there's the niche aspect. Knowing which theme suits you best may help you narrow down a niche; some possibilities include hospitals, airlines, kids' birthday parties, or corporate conferences with a healthy twist.

## *The Music Lover*

Ah, music. It touches all of our lives. Who doesn't have a favourite song, or three? Again, there are so many different ways that you can embrace a life centred on music. Teaching is an obvious and easy starter for creating your music-themed life, particularly if you're passionate about teaching, but also because it is easy to do it from home with minimal start-up costs (assuming you have your own instrument and a free corner) to give you a bit of an income as you build up your creator experience and profile.

As with food, you could start your own school if you're really ambitious; it could be specialist – woodwind only, say, or cover all possible instruments. Would you prefer one-on-one teaching, groups, adults or children? Maybe you'd love to be a music teacher in a school – it would give you that extra stability and security of income.

Are you, instead, hankering to play in front of audiences? How far do you want to go? Are you happy with your local pub, and maybe the odd corporate function or do you want to be a rock-and-roll star? Are you a solo artist or do you love being part of a group or band? Maybe orchestral work is your true calling? Do you write your own songs? Maybe folk festivals are more your scene? If you're a singer, what genre do you love – opera, pop, country, folk, jazz, blues, or heavy metal? Maybe you love the idea of musicals or musical theatre, or cabaret. Perhaps you're a composer or arranger, hankering to write a movie score, or you're a born conductor waiting for that call from the London Philharmonic?

Does the history or evolution of music through the ages interest you? Perhaps you would love to collect old – or recent – music manuscripts. Is there one composer or artist that you're passionate about? You could write histories of music or biographies of great composers, recent rock legends, or hitherto undiscovered or ignored long-gone musical geniuses waiting to be re-introduced to the world.

Again, travel is a possibility – creating tours focussing on a particular musician/composer, musical period or musical genre. You could be a music critic, travelling the world to report on the big shows, or just stick with your local city. Perhaps you are fascinated by particular types of musical instruments and collect and write about those. Do you love to experiment with different sounds through making your own instruments, or do you love creating beautiful instruments?

### The Nature Spirit

A passion like nature is a little different from food and music; it is difficult to imagine one-on-one lessons in nature, for example. So, what are the possibilities? Much of nature can be thought of as a "place", so travel comes immediately to mind. There is also the question of how adventurous you are. If you run tours, do you want to take people mountain climbing in the Himalayas or would you prefer hiking through the North American wilderness? Perhaps bike tours along quaint European country lanes would appeal to you. You could consider running camps for school groups to teach young people more about nature and the environment.

Writing about nature is a possibility – think National Geographic magazine. If you have an artistic bent you might want to photograph nature. There are, of course, plenty of study options available such as environmental engineering, veterinary science; if your interest in nature is more about animals than landscapes, horticulture; if your interest is more about gardening, or environmental management, conservation or forestry.

If you did want to teach, of course, you could consider geography, or more practical areas, such as ecology and environmental management. You could also consider becoming involved as a volunteer in organisations such as the Scouts. Perhaps farming would interest you: either animals, or crops, or both. A simple country cottage life might be what you're looking for, where self-sufficiency is your primary aim. You could have a vegetable garden, fruit trees and some chickens, maybe teaching others how to be self-sufficient using your garden as an example, even going on the speaker circuit to spread the word more widely, or compare self-sufficiency in the garden with success in the corporate world.

Maybe it's water that you love, which opens up a whole other raft of possibilities (excuse the pun). You could live on a houseboat. You could fish for a living, take others on fishing tours, or teach people to fish. You could become a marine biologist or take people on diving tours.

With just these three areas, you can see that the possibilities are endless! Whatever your broad area of interest, there will be a place for you in it that is as unique to you as you want it to be. You just need to be a little bit creative, have confidence in yourself and get started. Then watch more possibilities open up for you than you'll know what to do with!

## Chapter 5 Review

What's possible is limited only by your imagination. However, trying to come up with a vision for a dream life can be overwhelming. And often, we have hidden resistances holding us back. Taking some time to reflect on your life, where it is, where you'd like it to be, and why it isn't there, can provide you with some valuable insights into your hidden fears. However, even while you're working on your resistance, you can take some small, manageable steps to start you on your way.

It can be easier to break down your dream life, living your passion, and focus on one facet at a time, building it up and broadening your vision as you go. The framework given in Figure 2, along with the examples for food, music and nature, is one way to approach it. I am also a very big fan of mind-maps. Trying to work out how you would like to live your passion is a perfect use for a mind-map.

Throughout this book you'll come across different ways of finding your passion, if you don't know what it is, or narrowing down how to approach it if you do. As we said at the beginning of this chapter, the key is to take a step. I like to think of all steps as forward steps, even if they don't seem like it initially. It's like looking back to how you were as a teenager or even in your twenties (or thirties!) and cringing at how you behaved. Yes, you know better now – but that's only because you have had the experience of behaving in ways that didn't work. Life is one big experiment. You try things to see if they work and, if they don't, you try something different. Once you have narrowed in on what you really want to do, you can find a mentor, someone who has done what you want to do, so that you can copy their successful steps, avoiding the mistakes that they made, thereby achieving your goal sooner.

# Chapter 6

# What is Your Passion?

*"When I was 5 years old, my mother always told me that happiness was the key to life. When I went to school, they asked me what I wanted to be when I grew up. I wrote down 'happy'. They told me I didn't understand the assignment, and I told them they didn't understand life."*

JOHN LENNON

Ironically, the most significant obstacle to people living the life of their dreams is actually working out what the life of their dreams *is*. You need to have a vision to aspire to and the truth is that many people simply don't know where to start to find or develop one. So, most don't even make an attempt. The main reason for this, I believe, is because there is an unspoken expectation that your life will follow a particular, conveyor-belt like structure. This rigid structure includes going to school, doing some sort of post-school training, such as an apprenticeship or university, and getting a "good" job.

From the time you are small, you are asked the question, "What do you want to be when you grow up?" The "correct" answer is something tangible like, "a fireman" or "a nurse". There is no allowance for anything more esoteric. Even something like "an artist", which is a very tangible possibility, is generally frowned upon because of the perceived difficulty of making any, let alone enough, money at it. And, besides, it sounds like way too much fun. Who ever heard of having a career where you can be creative and have fun? That doesn't sound right at all! That's what the weekends are for. If you're lucky.

Schools also drum this into us from an early age. School generally tends to be rigid and structured. There is not much fun-having at all. Not even in art classes, as I recall, or in cooking classes. In two of the most creative pursuits you do at school, there is no fun. Well, maybe I'm being a little harsh, but I'm sure you get my point.

So, why is that? Why is there so little room for fun at school? There are always deadlines to be met, as you have to get to the next class on time, and you are constantly being judged and compared with your peers. The teachers have to give you a grade somehow, and they do this by measuring your performance. But what is it that they actually measure? It certainly isn't how much fun you had. (In fact, the more fun you had, the lower your grade is likely to be, given the way such classes are generally run.) It can be all very demoralising and does not allow for much in the way of real creativity, which is what humans are here to do – we create.

Some fortunate people, however, are able to break out of the "tangible career with a uniform so you can tell who I am" mindset and create a fun, love-filled and wealthy life for themselves. I say "who I am" on purpose as that is another problem – that we identify ourselves so much with *what we do*. You are not what you do. And the sooner you can wean yourself from the idea that "you are what you do" the more chance you'll have of creating a vision of a dream life for yourself.

Probably the most appropriate word for most such people is "entrepreneur". One online dictionary[1] definition I found for entrepreneur was "a person who organizes and manages any enterprise, especially a business, usually with considerable initiative and risk". You don't have to be an entrepreneur to create your dream life, but you do need to be able to think like one. That is, you need to be able to use some, or even considerable, initiative and creativity and you need to be comfortable with at least a moderate level of risk. Now, this is not because being entrepreneurial is fundamentally so scary or risky but because it is not the norm. Most of us don't have much exposure to entrepreneurs and how they work, so it doesn't seem as natural to most of us, as does working for an employer.

So, you may perceive that there is more risk in following your passion than if you followed a "standard" career path, even if there isn't really if you approach it in the right way. You will also almost certainly face a reasonable amount of opposition from others who don't understand what you are doing. They will

---
1   http://dictionary.com

tell you all of the things that *they* think could go wrong and all of the reasons why *they* think you should not do it. You do not need to listen to them – it is their fears coming out and their fears have nothing to do with you.

In the previous chapter we talked about what's possible with respect to living your dream life by following your passion, and gave several examples of the kinds of things you could do with a particular passion, such as food or music. There were plenty of ideas in these examples to inspire you and get you at least a little bit excited about the possibilities for yourself and how you would like to create your dream life. Right now, we're going to get stuck straight into discovering the things that get your heart soaring and your creativity flowing.

## *Pause for Thought #9: Passions and Values*

Once again take out your paper and pen and get ready for a journey through your interests and pastimes to start uncovering clues to your passions. The following questions are designed to give you some insights into what kinds of things, people, situations and activities tend to appeal to you – your passions and values. Your values are defined[2] as "principles or standards of behaviour; one's judgement of what is important in life". Your passions are defined2 as those things for which you have "an intense desire or enthusiasm".

I would even go further and say that your passions tend to be directed towards more tangible, objective things such as a particular activity (e.g. painting or bike riding), whereas your values are more intangible and subjective, as the words behaviour and judgement suggest. In this process you are, for now, looking for themes rather than specific details. Although, if any specific details really stand out for you, by all means, grab hold and run with them!

Answer each question below with the first thing that comes into your head. Feel free to write down more than one thing for each question as well. But don't think too much about it. Just write down each thing as it comes to you, don't force it. If you're struggling to come up with further answers, just move on to the next question.

1. If you knew that you would have the full support of everyone whose opinion you care about, or else they were no longer with us, and you knew you could fully support yourself financially, what would you choose to spend most of your time doing?

---

[2] http://oxforddictionaries.com/

2. What is your definition of fun? What do you do for fun, or what do you find fun?
3. What activity would you always do, even if you were not paid? What is it that appeals to you about this activity?
4. If you had all the money and all the time in the world, where would you visit? What is it that appeals to you about this place?
5. If you could have dinner with any person, living or dead, who would it be? What is it that appeals to you about this person? What is it that you would hope to learn from this person?
6. If you could be an expert at something, what would it be? What is it that appeals to you about this field or activity?
7. What is your favourite movie? What is it about this movie that appeals to you?
8. What is your favourite book? What is it about this book that appeals to you?
9. Who is your favourite movie character? What is it that appeals to you about them?
10. What courses have you done over the years? Include your final year at school if you think it is relevant, any tertiary education, workshops, short courses etc. Be as general or specific as you like. Which were your favourites? What about them appealed to you?
11. What are your hobbies? What are the things that appeal to you about these hobbies?
12. If you had a whole afternoon free, and you chose to spend it playing a game, what game would it be? Why?
13. If you had a whole afternoon free and you chose to do something creative, what would that be? Why?
14. What things come to mind when you think/say the word love?
15. What things come to mind when you think/say the word joy?
16. What things come to mind when you think/say the word truth?

Now, to really clarify the themes that are coming through, you are going to do a graphical representation of the ideas that have come up in answering the questions. I find mind-maps to be a very effective graphical representation tool, but use whichever tool or method is your favourite. Also make sure you have enough space to incorporate all of your ideas, as well as allowing for more that will pop up as you are creating your illustration. A white board or sheet of butcher's paper will work well.

Now consider the following with respect to your answers to the questions above and your mind-map.

- What themes are coming through in your mind-map? Are there a few strong ones, or one main one?
- Are you surprised? Or did it bring out what you already knew underneath but were never game enough to really see or take seriously as an option for making it your life's focus?
- Are there any that you would like to change? Or would you like to change the emphasis (stronger or weaker) of some?
- Prioritize those that you would like to focus on in your life, going down in order of importance.
- Take the first item on the list and brainstorm ways that you could change the emphasis of that theme/value in your life (maybe with another mind-map).
- Come up with a plan to integrate this into your life starting today.
- Repeat this process as often as you need to. Maybe try a new idea once a week or once a month.

Repeat the values process once every six to twelve months and compare with your answers from the previous time. If you have followed the above process, you should find that your activities and focus are moving in the direction indicated by your values and passions.

- If any that you would prefer to de-emphasize are staying the same or even increasing, you may wish to reflect on why this is. There may be some hidden resistance that is stopping this from changing, or else you might realise that there were some hidden fears or resistance that caused you to think that you wanted to de-emphasize these when it would actually be more appropriate and fulfilling for you to allow them more fully into your life.
- If any that you would prefer to emphasize further are staying the same or even decreasing, you may wish to consider why this is. Again, there may be some hidden resistance that is stopping this from changing, or it may be that you felt a subconscious obligation to emphasize these apparent values or passions when, in fact, you would be more fulfilled

by de-emphasizing them (because they actually don't fit in with your values or your passions at all).

Now, if you've really taken the time to answer the questions in this exercise and do the mind-map, and really reflect on just who you are and what floats your boat (as they say), you will have at least one really exciting idea, probably more, that you want to start exploring further. You'll want to know what steps you can take to start integrating this idea into your life or, even more excitingly, to start making big changes to your life! That's what we're going to talk about next.

## Now I Know Where I'm Going, But Where Do I Start?

I have always been a subscriber to the belief that if someone else can do it, so can I. I particularly remember using this philosophy at school. I somehow had an innate sense of it. You can apply this idea to anything that you want to do. And if no one else has done it before, you could use the argument that if you can think of it, there must be a way to achieve it – you just have to try enough different ways.

The Wright brothers found a way for humans to fly when no one had done it before. Sir Edmund Hillary and Tenzing Norgay were the first known people to climb to the peak of Mount Everest. NASA was the first to fly people to the moon when Neil Armstrong, Buzz Aldrin and Michael Collins succeeded in their mission in July 1969. Roger Bannister was the first person to break the four-minute mile. Each of these feats has been repeated many times since. Once these people proved that these feats could actually be achieved, others were able to believe that they, too, could achieve them – and did.

What you might notice, though, is that, generally, "new" things or achievements, including those mentioned above, are a culmination of many smaller steps building on the accomplishments of the previous steps. I saw an interview with Neil Armstrong where he humbly acknowledged that around 400,000 people helped to put him on the moon; he was just the guy who got to step onto the moon at the end of all of their efforts, and take all the glory. So, it was the putting together of the steps of 400,000 people, plus the steps of all of the people who developed the science and technologies that preceded the moon-landing project that enabled it to happen. It wasn't an overnight achievement.

The point here is that you don't have to go and work out everything for yourself. If you have a dream that you want to achieve, you just have to follow the steps of those who have gone before you and been successful in what you want to do. As Anthony Robbins says, "Success leaves clues." Find someone who has achieved what you want to achieve; find out how they did it, and copy what they did!

What if you're trying to do something a little bit different from what anyone else has tried? Perhaps you're embarking on a quite unique business idea. Find a business that is as close as possible to your idea, follow what the founders did as far as it matches your business and the next step should be a natural progression. If it feels like the next step is, instead, going to be a leap, maybe start with where you are and where you want to be and then break the difference down into smaller steps or goals. For example, if you wanted to create a business with $1 million in turnover per annum but you only managed $10,000 in your first year, maybe aim for $1 million in 5 or 10 years, and set intermediate goals for the intervening years. Then you can review these goals as you go along, updating your projections based on your actual turnover figures each year.

One of the problems for you might be a matter of resources. Even if you do know exactly the steps to follow to establish your dream business, you might have no money to spare as you have a mortgage and a cat to support and, therefore, can't leave your current job. I would bet that you're not the first person to have had this problem. Richard Branson certainly didn't start out rich – but he was creative and passionate, and he used his initiative. You could find someone who started out equally poor and find out how they raised the money. You don't just have to find one person to model. You can find a different person for each step.

I would suggest you start with finding someone who has achieved your big goal (e.g. dream business, or close to it). You need to find out what the *crucial* steps were. Did they need to have their own premises to really get things going? Did they realise it was better to be situated in a particular part of town; the industrial part or the restaurant quarter, for example? Did they need a big cash injection right at the start – perhaps due to requiting equipment? Do as much research and find out as much detail as you can. Some good places to start include company websites, business magazines and biographies.

What about finances? Do you have the finances you need to get started, or do you need some outside help? Do you have family and friends who are willing and able to lend you money to help you to get started, or do they usually ask you for money? If you don't have the money to get started, and don't have friends or family willing or able to help you out, you'll have to get creative about finding other sources. It might mean really tightening your belt and saving up for a year or two. It might mean taking on a second or third job for a while. Or else, it might mean getting out there and promoting your idea to attract some other willing investors.

There are groups of people, such as angel investors, who specifically look for start-up businesses to invest in. Before you approach such people you'll need to have an excellent pitch to convince them that they're onto a winner with you. Again, look to others who have travelled this route for inspiration. What arguments or incentives did they use to convince others to invest in them and their idea? Find an appropriate model and you're well on your way – no matter what step you're up to in creating your dream life.

## *I Have a Vague Idea, but I Want More Clarity*

Zig Ziglar said, "You don't have to see the whole staircase; you just have to take the first step." In other words, don't be paralysed by not knowing exactly what it is that you want to achieve, if you're still not 100% clear. If you at least know that you're passionate about a particular area, just do something, take some action that will allow you to explore this passion in greater detail, and the exciting possibilities that it holds. The idea is that by experiencing a lot of different stuff, you will gradually home in on what you like to do, what really fires you up, and a more concrete way of bringing this into your life will start to form in your head.

The message here, then, is to not worry about "what you want to be when you grow up" if it isn't obvious to you right now. Just do something that you really enjoy doing or that you think you will really enjoy doing. Give yourself a task to complete that fits in with what you do know of your passion. This may be completing a degree, creating a sculpture, writing a book, or travelling through South America for a year. As you're accomplishing that task, look out for what reveals itself along the way, to give you clues about what to focus on next.

If you find that things that you do try actually don't interest you so much, then that is useful information too. If you can pinpoint what you don't like, it may be another clue as to what you would like. After you've taken a few steps along this path, a pattern will start to emerge. You will find that there has been a common thread through all of the things you have tried, or at least amongst all of the things that you liked. You may even find that you have an "Aha! moment" and gain a much clearer idea of where you want to go next – and possibly want to do for the rest of your life, or at least for the foreseeable future. You never know what else you might discover in the years to come. If you don't have that "Aha!" that's okay – you just have more experiencing to do.

What you want to be when you grow up should be an evolution of understanding as you experience more of life, grow as a person, and understand more of what the world has to offer – and what you have to offer it back. Even when you do think you know your passion and your life's purpose, it's okay for this to change and evolve. It will evolve naturally anyway, as you refine your understanding and knowledge.

So don't hold yourself back because you haven't resolved the "what you want to be when you grow up" mystery. Just start doing something that you love or really enjoy. If you haven't been doing this, start now no matter whether you're eighteen or eighty. Why would you spend another minute doing stuff that you don't love?

## *Pause for Thought #10: Who Do You Want to Be?*

Essential to living a happy life is knowing and being the kind of person that you want to be. That's what you're going to explore now. I have purposely put this exercise after the "what you want to focus on" exercise because I think having some insights into what you want to focus on will really help you to determine what kind of person you want to be. That is, you will want to be the kind of person who focusses on the kinds of things you worked out you want to focus on! Of course, it won't necessarily be as straight forward as that. And that is okay. You will almost certainly find that different ideas will come up during this process that will feed back into the previous process and so on. All you need to do, then, is to go back to your mind-map and add (and maybe delete) some pictures, words or links to fit in the new insights you have gained.

In this exercise, the idea is to think about, and write down, what you would *like* people to say at your funeral or, as it is often referred to these days, the Celebration of Your Life. This is not about what you *think* they will say. So, you are going to write your obituary. If you haven't done this process before, it is a very powerful process which should be repeated regularly.

Now, I want you to imagine your funeral. Imagine it *however* you would like it to be (maybe it is a State funeral). Imagine each of the following people, in turn, standing up to talk about their experience of you during your life. It is a good idea to keep in mind the six human needs, discussed in Chapter 3. It does not matter which one or ones you want to be driven by, but your answers to the following should be congruent with it or them. You may find it easier to just use dot points for your answers.

1. A work colleague
2. A good friend
3. A family member
4. An intimate partner
5. Your child
6. A stranger who knows of you or your life's contributions

Now, similarly to the previous exercise, I want you to look back over all of the points you have written down. Consider the following questions, with respect to your answers.

- Are there any themes here?
- Do you feel that it would be possible for people to say any of these things about you now? If so, which ones?
- Which things do you feel that it would be impossible for anyone to say about you now, or at least unlikely that they would?
- Prioritize your answers starting with the ones you would most like people to say about you, going down in order of importance.
- Take the first item in this list and brainstorm (you could start a new mind-map if you wish, or even incorporate the ideas into the one you did above) some ways you could start being the kind of person that others would say this about. You may find that you are already doing some of these things. If so, try to think of ways you could expand on these things.
- Come up with a plan to integrate this into your life, starting today.

Repeat this process as often as you need to. Maybe try a new idea once a week or once a month. As you start incorporating new ideas into your life and becoming the kind of person that you really want to be, the kind of person who does the things that you are passionate about, you will find your happiness increasing. Life will take on a whole new feel and meaning. Yes, you will still have problems to solve because no matter what we do we have "problems" – that is what life is about. However, you will have better quality problems, problems that, when solved, will enrich your life and lead you to even better quality problems. And they won't seem such a problem anymore – they will be part of the joy that is your life.

## What's the Next Step?

You now know at least one thing that you're passionate about and that you want to start or increase your focus on from *today*. And you should have a good idea of the kind of person you want to be while you are focussing on it. Let's have a look at some examples to give you some inspiration.

## Luke's Story

Luke had had a comfortable childhood and, if anything, had been a little overindulged by his mother. This led to him growing up to take things a little bit too much for granted and to not be as tolerant of others as he could have been. One day on his way to work he stopped in at the newsagent to buy a newspaper and realised that he had forgotten his wallet. He was rather disappointed because his football team had won the grand final the day before and he wanted to see the coverage in all its glory, splashed over the front page. He was also rather embarrassed because he didn't realise that he had forgotten his wallet until he got to the counter and the shop assistant had already rung up the sale.

As he explained his predicament and went to put the newspaper back, the customer behind him piped up and said, "Excuse me, I'll pay for it, if you like." Luke initially refused, but the woman insisted and Luke agreed, thanking her profusely. He hastily left the shop with his newspaper and went to work. But he thought about the woman's kindness all day. He asked himself if he would have done the same for someone else. He acknowledged to himself that he probably wouldn't have. In fact, he probably would have been annoyed with them for being so careless and for holding him up. After all, he was busy and important, and had things to do.

Some months later, when Luke came to do the obituary exercise, he remembered the woman's kindness and found that it had had such a profound effect on him that he wanted to include being kind more into his own life and way of being. It showed up as a significant theme in his answers to the questions and he decided to make it his first value to focus on. On reflecting on how he could start to introduce kindness every day into his life, he realised that he didn't have to wait for people to be in distress before he could perform an act of kindness, he could take some initiative. He decided that the simplest way to start was to smile at people more. He started with setting a goal of smiling at ten different people each day (that is, he could only count a smile at any one person more than once if he saw them on different days).

Then he realised that he could be more openly appreciative of the work that others did, even if it was "part of their job". He began being more observant of what his co-workers did and praising them – at all levels – for anything appropriate. He was careful not to be false or disingenuous. For example, when he knew that one of his co-workers had done a lot of work on a report, he made sure to mention it in a meeting with senior staff present; whereas in the past, he would have assumed that everyone knew the work the co-worker had done and it wouldn't have occurred to him to say anything, just to discuss the content, with little thought to the work put in.

If he found someone else's document at the printer, he would take it to them at their desk. He also started making more of an effort to ask about his co-workers' families and home-life. It's not that he spent hours at the water cooler, he made sure that this didn't take up more than 10 or 15 minutes on any given day, but he noticed after a relatively short time, that people were becoming much kinder to him in return and he found that he looked forward to going to work more than in the past. It became more about the people he was working with and a little less about "just getting the job done", which doesn't necessarily make you more productive in the short or long term – after all, it is interacting with others that can bring out the best ideas. It wasn't that he hadn't enjoyed his work previously; he had, it was just that he hadn't realised how much better it could be.

## Jen's Story

Jen was an accountant working in a relatively large firm. She had always done quite well at school and her parents had strongly encouraged her to do something that would get her a good job, something respectable, and accounting was particularly acceptable to them. She had done the normal things at school, playing netball on the weekends and working at a part-time job after school, and had then gone straight on to university, particularly as her parents were afraid she might not go back if she took time off. She was fortunate enough to get a graduate position with a large, reputable company at the end of her degree and was still working for the same company six years later.

In her private life, Jen had had one boyfriend during her university years, until he had broken her heart. Then a year after she had started working, she met Scott and they had been seeing each other ever since. Two years previously, they had moved in together and then over the last summer they had gone to Europe on an organised tour through nine countries. It had been Jen's first trip overseas. During their trip to Paris, when they were at the top of the Eiffel Tower, Scott had proposed. Jen had said yes. However, even though that was now six months ago, she had been unable to set a date. Somehow she couldn't bring herself to do it. Scott was becoming impatient with her, and she was wondering what was wrong with her.

To help her to sort out her disinclination to set a date, she undertook the passions and values exercises, above. The major themes that came up for Jen were that she yearned for more excitement in her life and that she particularly valued courage. She realised that she had led such a sheltered, cossetted life that she had practically never had to step outside her comfort zone. And when she had, she had actually been pretty well cushioned. For example, her first overseas trip was to Western countries, she was accompanied by Scott whom she knew intimately, and it was on an organised tour, so she didn't have to work out any details for herself. She had also followed what her parents had expected for her study and career, having had a strong sense of being the dutiful daughter.

The outcomes of the exercises made Jen realise that the reason she had been reticent to set a date to marry Scott was not that she didn't love him, as she had been afraid it might mean, but that she was terrified that the rest of her life might continue to be as predictable, and as much in the vein of meeting others' expectations, as it had been up until now. She needed to step out and really find out who she was, test herself, try some different things.

Jen talked over what she had discovered about herself with Scott, who was disappointed but supportive. Over the next few weeks, Jen searched for and found a volunteering opportunity in Ecuador at an orphanage. She had been very good with her money and had saved quite a lot since she had started working (that accounting degree had brought some good, after all). She had enough to support herself for at least twelve months. On talking with her boss, who was surprised but also supportive, Jen was offered twelve months' leave without pay. While Jen appreciated this offer, it did, after all, mean that her employer valued her, she wanted to quit her job. She felt that it was important for her personal growth that she didn't have a safety net to come back to.

Scott went to visit Jen about six months into her time away. It was quickly clear to both of them that Jen had changed and was not the same person that Scott had fallen in love with and that Jen needed things that Scott could not provide. Jen was sad when Scott left to go back home, but she knew she had done the right thing. And if she hadn't done this now, she was fairly sure that these latent needs for excitement and acting with courage would have come up sooner or later, perhaps after they'd had children, and the situation would have been a lot more complicated. At least she did not have to live with regret.

Over the next several years, Jen took up different posts with the same and different aid organisations, moving into paid positions, and making her way up the ladder to oversee aid efforts in particular regions. She met her need for excitement through her constant travel, meeting new people from various cultures, and seeing new and interesting places. Her job often required courage when dealing with sometimes dangerous situations in war-torn areas. And she did eventually marry a fellow aid worker, who had a similar love for adventure and helping those in need.

## Chapter 6 Review

Finding something that you are passionate about, that you can turn into your life's purpose, is a joy that no one should be denied. Until you find your passion or passions, you might feel like you are wandering around life in a bit of a daze. Something does not feel right, but you may be so used to the feeling that you don't even realise it is there. You might find yourself wondering what it's all about; what's the point of it all? When you discover that you have a passion and you allow it to take hold of you and evolve into a dream, you don't wonder anymore. Your dream is what it's all about. Your life has a point, a meaningful purpose, and you never, ever look back.

There will still be ups and downs, and probably some running around in circles. There will be tears, and tantrums, and feet-stomping. However, there will also be a lot more joy, and laughter, and dancing about. How, I hear you asking? When you find your passion and then your purpose, you're way more open to being inspired by new possibilities and opportunities, pushing you ever forward. You'll attract other passionate people through your enthusiasm and zest, inspiring them and creating more joy through connection and more opportunities. Life will never be the same again.

# Chapter 7

# Intuition – The GPS for Your Life

*"Until you make the unconscious conscious, it will direct your life and you will call it fate."*

CARL JUNG

Your intuition, also often called your "gut-feeling", is one of the few aspects in the realm of the sixth sense that is generally accepted as existing and a useful tool. The term "women's intuition" has been around for centuries, although of course men have it too. Once you know how to interpret its subtleties and nuances, this inner GPS will never get you lost – unlike many commercial ones. It can be used to your advantage in all kinds of situations.

Intuition is your inner guide to your life and your path. You could think of it in terms of what your subconscious mind has picked up that your conscious mind hasn't. It is said that our senses take in many millions of bits of information every second. If our brains did not filter out some of this information, we would literally go insane because it would be so overwhelming. However, just because it has been filtered from our consciousness, it does not necessarily mean that it has been flushed from our minds altogether. The tool that we call intuition is simply an amplifier for the information in your subconscious. While it is not clear how it works, physically, I believe it is a combination of tapping into deeply buried memories and picking up on energies that our other senses do not. It's as if it actually is a sense for energy, for example from the people around you – happy, scared, threatening – a sixth sense.

## Why Is It Useful?

I remember the first time I really became aware of my intuition. I was 13. I had been chosen in a try-out squad for a representative netball team. After the final try-outs, I was chosen as the goal shooter. I had made the squad. When I got home that night, I was trying to enjoy the feeling of having made the squad but something was stopping me. I had a gut-feeling that it wasn't right but I couldn't figure out why. We had definitely had the final try-outs. There was no logical reason for me to believe there was a problem. But I had a nagging feeling that I couldn't "count my chickens" just yet – even though every physical piece of evidence that I had said that my chickens had well and truly hatched and were alive and well!

The following week when I went along to training, another girl spoke up, saying she hadn't had a chance to try out the previous week. She was also a goal shooter. It wasn't clear why she hadn't spoken up the previous week, but she was given a try-out. I was not playing my best. She was better than me. She got the position and I was no longer in the squad. Maybe my subconscious had noticed the girl who didn't get a try-out at the official final try-outs the week before. Maybe it noticed her in the background and noticed her distress. While I was obviously very disappointed, it was an invaluable experience which awakened me to the power of my intuition and how useful a guide it could be in making decisions and making provisional plans with respect to otherwise unanticipated outcomes.

From a spiritual point of view, many people believe that your intuition is the voice of your spirit or soul, giving you guidance from "the beyond" (as Professor Trelawney calls it in the "Harry Potter and the Prisoner of Azkaban" movie). I actually love this explanation because, if this is the case, how could you not trust it? Surely your spirit knows what is best for you? It can definitely see the bigger picture since it is not limited to your physical body or senses.

Regardless of where you believe your intuition comes from, you can view it simply as that inner sensation you get at certain times that can act as a guide as to how best to respond to what is happening. You can learn to tune in to it, to become more aware of it. I rely on it all the time for helping me to make decisions, big and small. An example of something small is if I want to comment on something to someone else, possibly someone I am not completely comfortable with. If my intuition tells me that my comment is not going to go down well, I don't say it.

For example, consider Jane talking to her subordinate colleague Kate about how she had just met a new colleague, Anita, and saying how nice Anita seemed. Anita had been hired at the same level as Kate. However, Kate had also met Anita earlier and had found her to be rude. In fact Anita had been quite dismissive of Kate and, it seemed to Kate, had only been interested in being nice to those she was introduced to who had positions at a higher level than her own. In other words, Kate thought Anita was inclined to be a bit of a workplace social climber.

Kate considered making a comment to this effect to Jane who, although being at a higher level, she knew quite well. However, her intuition told her that, on this occasion, saying something would not be well-received by Jane. So, she chose to keep quiet. Now, it may seem obvious that Kate should have kept her thoughts to herself in this situation. Maybe Anita hadn't meant to be rude and Kate had misinterpreted her behaviour due to her own insecurity issues. She had, after all, only just met Anita and perhaps she was nervous as it was her first day and she should give her more time. On the other hand, though, she may have often discussed office politics with Jane and so it may not have been wildly out of place for her to make such an observation. Also, she may have been quite hurt by Anita's response to her and her emotions may have reared up wanting to be heard. I'm sure we've all had this experience on occasion.

Now, in this example, even if Kate had chosen to ignore her intuition and make a disparaging comment about Anita to Jane, as they knew each other reasonably well, the consequences would probably have been no more than Jane admonishing Kate and pointing out to her that it was only Anita's first day and that she was probably nervous. Kate would have felt a bit silly for a while and that would have been the end of it. But, starting by listening to your intuition in small situations like this, where the consequences of getting it wrong are minimal, is excellent practice for the bigger stuff.

*Intuitive Response Versus Emotional Response*

I admit it has taken me many years to consistently listen to this inner voice. In the past I let my emotions take over. If, for example, what the other person was saying pressed my buttons, I would get that instant knee-jerk response in my gut and need (or so I thought) to blurt out whatever then came into my head. Or else, if I was chatting to someone and a funny comment (well, I thought it was funny...) came into my head, or else I felt passionately about what they were saying and wanted to add my two-bits worth, I found it difficult to keep it to myself.

Our emotions are very strong motivators. However, having not listened to that inner voice often enough, and having had my joke fall flat, or my passionate retort be scorned or dismissed by the person I was talking to, I finally learned to listen to that inner voice. In fact it wasn't until I started listening to that inner voice that I realised that what I had been doing was allowing my emotions to take over.

Now, I am all for allowing your emotions to be expressed when appropriate but, unfortunately, they are not always your best guide. They are particularly dangerous when they arise because of your buttons being pressed, as this is an indication of a remnant issue, probably from childhood, for which expressing those emotions may have been appropriate at the time the issue arose, but doing so now is not likely to be serving you so well. Even if you aren't aware of any such childhood issues (and, believe me, we ALL have them to one degree or another), tuning in to your intuition is one way of helping you to avoid the often embarrassing and possibly long-term consequences of such inappropriate reactions.

On the other hand, there have also been times when my intuition has told me that the interaction would go well. At such times it has given me the confidence to go ahead with my intended response, perhaps when I am "testing" if another person has the same sense of humour as me, and it has gone well. Of course, you could also argue that it went well because I believed it would and the confidence that imbued in me. It doesn't really matter how you look at it. If you get even a hint of a feeling, go with it. I haven't gone wrong when I have listened to it. And listening to it is the key.

This brings me to another point, though, and that is that your intuition is largely about how you will *feel* about what happens, rather than whether or not what happens is actually "good" or "bad". This is good news because then you have a choice about the outcome – at least in terms of how you feel about it. And this is, of course, because you have control over how you feel about things, always. Really, you could argue, then, that this does actually give you control over the outcome because, so often, we let how we feel dictate how we behave.

So, if we can be forewarned (by tapping into our intuition early enough) of how we will feel given our current attitude to the situation, if we have enough time and/or control over our feelings, we can change the outcome of a given situation, compared to what our intuition initially told us. That is, it is a guide to how we will feel about a situation given how everything currently is and the direction things are taking. It is not necessarily set in stone.

## *What Does Your Intuition Feel Like?*

Your intuition can take on many forms, some that may be unique to you. Generally, however, your intuition will manifest itself in one of three ways. One, you will get a quick, "jabbing" feeling. I generally feel this in the area from my heart to my solar plexus. This can be a positive or a negative feeling and is generally reasonably strong, indicating intensity of emotion. That is, either the event is going to go excitingly well or else it is going to go disappointingly badly. You will usually be able to tell the difference. If your intuition manifests as a jabbing sensation, it is generally an indication that there is an element of surprise in the outcome; something that you were not expecting, either positive or negative. If positive, it could still be something that you were hoping for but were not able to believe could be possible.

The second possibility is that you will feel a more measured, stable feeling. This could be a nice, simmering glow, indicating that things will go well. Or it could be a slight feeling of dread or disappointment, obviously indicating that things may not go so well, or at least not how you had hoped. This more measured feeling is generally an indication that there will be no great surprises. I find this kind of feeling generally comes up for situations or events where I know what the likely possible set of outcomes could be but it is not clear which particular one is the most likely. For example, you could be having a performance review meeting with your boss. Ideally, if the communication lines are good in your workplace, there will be no surprises at such meetings. However, communications are not always as good as we would like them to be, so your intuition would be really useful here.

Another difference between getting the "jab" kind of feeling and the more measured feeling is how attached you are to the outcome. For example, if you're playing in a sports grand final and you try to tune in to the result, you are more likely to get the "jab" sensation than the measured one, because there is more emotion involved – it is likely that you're pretty excited and would really like to win – and it's that kind of attitude that would have got you to the grand final in the first place. On the other hand, say you're walking past a bookshop and it occurs to you to see if they have the book you've been thinking of buying for a couple of months. While you would like to have the book, otherwise you wouldn't be looking for it, if it's been a couple of months, you're probably not strongly attached to the outcome of today's search. In this case, you're more likely to experience the measured sensation around whether or not the book will be in this shop than the "jab".

There is a third possibility. That is, that you may not feel anything much at all. There are two likely reasons behind this. The first is that you may be *too attached* to the outcome and your emotions are getting in the way. When you are overly attached to a particular outcome, you want that outcome so strongly that you effectively block out or "jam" (to use a telecommunications term), your intuition. You also can't (or won't let yourself) trust any intuitive feelings that you do get because you will tell yourself you're making them up – particularly if it has a hint of feeling the opposite to the outcome you want! If you feel negatively in such a situation, you will tell yourself that it is fear – and it could well be. If you feel positively, you will tell yourself that it's just your excitement and you won't trust it. In such circumstances, you need to calm yourself as much as possible, and sense the underlying feeling.

The second reason that you may not feel much at all is because there may not be any particular outcome at all. That is, your experience may be neither particularly positive, nor particularly negative, so there is no particular message to be gained from intuiting it. For example, you may have chosen to focus on getting your morning coffee. If you do this every morning and you are comfortable with the person you buy the coffee from, you basically have a routine, it is likely that you will feel nothing intuitive at all. We'll discuss these different possibilities in more detail further on in the chapter.

### *Pause for Thought #11: Tapping into Your Intuition*

So how do you tap into, or develop, your intuition? Here is an exercise that you can try. You can do this exercise almost anywhere, though it is best if you have some time to yourself, even just a few minutes. You could be sitting on the train on the way to work, or even driving to work (though it's perhaps best to just do it at the traffic lights—when your car is stationary, if you're the driver). The main thing is that you are not specifically communicating with anyone else.

- *Think about your day ahead*. What are the events that you know are, or that are likely to be, coming up in your day? Choose one to focus on. It can be as small as you like. It might even be buying your first morning coffee. However, it is preferable, and more useful, if it is an event that you are at least slightly uncertain or anxious about. Perhaps it is a meeting with a new client, or you need to negotiate something with a colleague.

- *Once you have chosen your event, focus on it.* Think about what you want to say or how you are planning to act. Then see what feelings you notice around your heart/solar plexus area. Are they positive or negative? Weak or strong? Is there a nice flowing feeling or did you get a jab? How would you interpret the feelings you got? Try to be as objective as possible.

One way you can use your intuition when you become more in-tune with it is to compare your intuitive responses to different potential scenarios. For example, if you have a meeting coming up with a subordinate in which you need to have a difficult discussion with them about their poor performance, you may be trying to decide whether it is best to take a softly-softly approach or a more hard-nosed, buck-'em-up kind of approach. By taking some time to yourself to focus on the situation and the two different approaches in turn, you may be able to get an intuitive sense of which will work better.

## *You Can't Force It*

While tuning in to your intuition can be incredibly useful, trying too hard to get an intuitive insight into how a situation or event will turn out can be counter-productive. This usually occurs when it is something for which you are strongly emotionally attached to the outcome. In such situations it is best to sit quietly and still your mind for several minutes. Focus on your breathing, as in meditation. Have the event of interest in the back of your mind and allow the feelings to flow.

With practice you will be able to tune in to the underlying feeling in your heart/solar plexus region. If you can't feel anything or can't make sense of what you are feeling, it is best to leave it until later, if there is time. You cannot force your intuition to be clear. Having to force it is actually an indication of being too emotionally attached to the outcome, which causes all kinds of trouble for your intuition. If you can let go of the issue for a while, it might actually allow your intuition to show up when you're just absent-mindedly thinking about the issue at a later time.

In fact, often the strongest and most accurate flashes of intuition occur out of the blue. They take you by surprise. You can be thinking about something, or someone, absent-mindedly and you will feel the intuitive "jabbing" sensation. I have generally experienced this in a positive way, but it could also be negative. For example, again as a teenager I was thinking about a boy I had a crush on (as we all do when we're teenagers – or girl, depending on your preference). All of a sudden I had a lovely positive flow of feeling in the heart/solar plexus area which was more than the longing slightly achy feeling you get when you think of someone you're not sure you can be with. It actually lasted several seconds. I knew that this meant that this boy would become my boyfriend – and soon – which he did.

Something I have found, though, is that intuition appears to be a very short-term indicator. That is, it is good at indicating the immediate outcome of a particular event or situation, but it does not seem to be applicable long-term. So, you may get a positive feeling about a particular meeting with a new client, for example. But that doesn't mean that the long-term relationship with that client will be all smooth-sailing, or even that it will eventuate to anything at all. So, while intuition can be a useful short-term indicator, and helpful in calming you down (if you get a positive response) for a particular event, it is not generally useful long-term.

However, far from being disappointing, this actually makes sense for several reasons. I am a believer in taking a step towards a long-term big goal, even if you're not sure what the step after that will be, as we discussed in the previous chapter. If you trust and allow things to unfold with the first step, the next step that you need to take will reveal itself in time. Further, if you believe in free will, then the future is largely not predictable, beyond a certain time limit, the length of which varies depending on the situation and the momentum behind it.

So, for example, even though I got a lovely feeling about the boy I had a crush on as a teenager and ended up having him as my boyfriend, that didn't mean that the relationship was going to last forever, or even result in marriage. As it was, it only lasted for about a year and a half – it turned out that we weren't so great for each other after all. So my intuition told me about the next step, but it didn't tell me the whole story. And, can you imagine if you did get the whole story for every situation? You'd be a mass of changing feelings (every relationship, for example, has its ups and downs, if that's what you're intuiting about) that would leave you feeling totally confused – and probably be unlikely to want to get into it in the first place! So, intuition is a useful "next step" indicator, and that's probably about as much as we could reasonably be expected to cope with.

Once you become more attuned to your intuition you will find that it is in almost constant flow as you become more and more sensitive to it. You are constantly aware of a feeling between your heart and your solar plexus which you can tap into at any time by simply focussing on whatever it is that you want an answer to or clarification on. The best time is when you feel "in the flow" – when you have a sense of knowing what to do next and your intuition feels quietly excited and confident without being overwhelming or exhausting, as it would if you were excited about something and had the adrenalin pumping. Being in the flow is gentler than that and provides you with ongoing energy rather than energy for now but causing you to feel spent later – like a sugar hit.

## *What if My Intuition Says Something Bad Is Going to Happen?*

We all know that things don't always go as we'd like them to, regardless of whether we believe that how they go is actually in our best interests. So, what do you do when your intuition tells you that something is not going to go well? Well, that is going to depend somewhat on the circumstances and how attached you are to having a positive outcome. At the very least, it may allow you to be prepared for a negative outcome. However, this can be dangerous, or at least a waste of energy, if the negative feeling actually refers to something else, perhaps something you have not considered or have overlooked.

Let's step back a bit and look at the bigger picture of "good" and "bad". I am a big fan of the idea that there is ultimately no "good" or "bad", there is just experience. This is an idea I first came across in Neale Donald Walsch's *Conversations With God* books, which I can highly recommend. I particularly loved the way that God, in these books, expressed a complete lack of judgement of anything that any of us could possibly do. All lives are equally valuable to the whole, no matter how they are lived. It is all experience gained for the greater good. He offers some lovely insights into how we can change the way we look at life by accepting everything as simply an experience. Good and bad are simply *labels* we give to situations or things in our lives that turn out, or not, as we had hoped. This is because we assume that we always know what is best for us. So, when things don't go as we had hoped, we label that as "bad".

However, I actually do believe that, subconsciously at least, we do know what is best for us. In this context, what is best for us does not always make us happy in the short term, but allows us to face and, ideally, master a particular life lesson. For example, I will bet that you know someone who keeps making the same relationship mistakes over and over; maybe it is even you? They keep going out with the same kind of person and the relationship lasts maybe a year, maybe two, it ends and then soon they find someone else who is almost a clone (at least in behaviour) of the other partners, or perhaps even worse.

*Pause for Thought #12: Using Your Intuition to Change Your Perspective*

So, back to the question of what to do if you get a negative intuitive response when you've tuned in to your intuition to get the inside scoop on something coming up for you. If you have enough time prior to the actual situation/event occurring, it is worthwhile sitting down and reflecting on the situation. Ask yourself the following questions (If you don't have time prior, it can also be useful to consider the following questions afterwards.):

- What would the ideal outcome be?
    - Why do you think this?
    - Write down all of the positives of this apparently ideal outcome.
    - Write down as many negatives as you had positives, of this outcome occurring.
- If the outcome isn't exactly as you hope, what is the most likely alternative outcome?
    - How is this not as "good" as the ideal outcome?
    - Write down all of the negatives of this outcome occurring.
    - Write down as many positives as you had negatives, of this outcome occurring.
    - What might the lesson be for you if this is the outcome that eventuates?
- What is the worst possible outcome scenario, as you currently see it?
    - Why do you think this?
    - Write down all of the negatives of this outcome occurring.
    - Write down as many positives as you had negatives, of this outcome occurring.
    - What might be the lesson, or lessons, for you if this is the outcome that eventuates?

Going through the above exercise, if you do it thoroughly enough, will give you a different perspective on the whole situation. If you can accept that the "good" and "bad" in every situation is simply your perception, usually based on a whole bunch of underlying assumptions that you probably aren't even aware of or else haven't admitted to yourself, you will begin to see the value in all situations and outcomes. You effectively become more of an observer of events and situations in your life, rather than getting caught up in all of the drama. That is not to say that you should sit idly as life passes you by, or "happens" to you, but such an approach will allow you to more readily tap into your intuition which will allow you to appreciate the lessons more readily. Such an approach will also allow you to be happier, as you learn to become less attached to particular outcomes and, instead, be more in the flow of life.

One of the reasons people get into the same relationship (or other life-situation) patterns time and time again is because they let their emotions, often underpinned by neediness or insecurity, take over and their intuition gets pushed into the background. When you learn to rely on your intuition as a guide, you effectively have access to an instruction manual which gives you step-by-step instructions on each situation you come across. As you become more and more in-tune with your intuition, the instruction manual becomes clearer and clearer. Instead of seeming to have been written by a native Japanese speaker who speaks and writes English badly, it starts to sound more like a native speaker with reasonable communication skills, though occasionally inebriated, until it finally reaches the level of the winner of the Nobel prize in literature.

At first glance, using your highly-tuned intuition as your step-by-step guide to everything almost seems like cheating. It's like sitting an exam and having someone looking over your shoulder telling you the answers – or at least telling you if your answer is right or wrong. However, what if you think of it like an open-book exam? When I was a student, and then a lecturer, I know many students preferred open-book exams, assuming that they were easier than closed-book (memory-based) exams. Many assumed that you'd need to do much less preparation and have less understanding of the material to successfully sit a closed-book exam. However, this is rarely the case.

To successfully navigate an open-book exam, you need to be organised, familiar with the material in the references available to you, and know how to interpret it and use it appropriately. Because you have reference material available to you, examiners can make the questions more complex. That is, they are inclined to ask questions that rely more on an understanding of the material rather than a regurgitation of facts (that can easily be looked up in the reference material you have with you). And it is the same when using your intuition.

Firstly, you need to be aware of it (organised), then you need to be familiar with it (know whether it is positive – what you want – or negative – what you don't want; strong or weak) and how to interpret it and use it appropriately (be able to interpret what it is telling you, as it relates to the situation/event in question). Your intuition is a part of who you are, whether you believe it is just your physical subconscious or your spirit. So if you can learn how to use it to help you to navigate your way through life, that is putting the magnificent being that is you to the best possible use and using it to its fullest potential.

As we so often stumble blindly about trying to work out why we keep getting into the same situation – if we actually even recognise this – often what's obvious to everyone else completely passes us by – having an inner guide gives us clues to when to question what is going on and our planned responses to it.

### *What if My Intuition is Cloudy?*

Many times when you try to tap into your intuition, the feeling can be non-distinct or cloudy. This can mean a number of things, as we briefly touched on above. Most often I have found that it simply means the obvious – that what will happen will be of little or no consequence to you; it will be – in your perception – neither good nor bad. You can think of it as a neutral outcome. It could also be that the situation you're contemplating will not come to fruition. Perhaps you're anticipating a confrontation with your boss but she/he turns out to be away that day. Or else, perhaps you had made a number of assumptions about how your boss would feel about and react to a given situation, but, in actual fact, they hadn't thought twice about it and didn't feel the need to discuss it with you at all.

Another possibility is that you are too attached to the outcome and so your emotions are blocking or crowding out your intuition. It's similar to the interference you hear sometimes when listening to the radio. I find if I have my mobile phone too close to my bedside clock-radio, for example, a buzzing will occur once an hour (if the radio is on) as the phone sends out a signal to the base station to update its location. So, as mentioned above, you can think of your emotional signals as interfering with your intuitive signals. In this case, it might be worth asking yourself the reflection questions from above for when you get a negative intuitive response.

A non-distinct intuitive feeling can also be an indication that you are barking up the wrong tree. Maybe the situation you're focussing on, trying to intuit, is not what you should be spending your energy on at this time. Consider

Imogen, who is interested in Dale, a co-worker she's known for a year or so now. They seem to get along quite well, but they really only see each other at morning coffee time, as they work in different sections. They have had a few chats and talk easily, but it is only ever for five to ten minutes at a time. She does know that he doesn't have a girlfriend, though, because he has spoken about a relationship breaking up eight months ago.

She tries to tap into her intuition to see whether or not they will become a couple but can't get anything solid, either positive or negative. The next week, Dale goes on holiday for four weeks, so that when he gets back there is more distance between them. A week after that, he gets moved to a different department on a different floor, and she rarely ever sees him. She doesn't have the courage to go and ask him out after such little contact – and such a lack of a show of interest from him – and her interest eventually fizzles out. A couple of months later, she meets someone else at a dinner party and Dale is all but forgotten. So, Dale was really a non-event.

Now if, instead, she had chosen to be courageous and ask Dale out herself, she may have had a strong negative feeling when she tried to intuit what would happen. Or, who knows, maybe it would have been strongly positive – maybe Dale wasn't sure whether she was interested in him and was waiting for her to ask him out! I'm pretty convinced, though, that your intuition is your best guide. Whether it's your sub-conscious or your spirit, if either had picked up on any interest from Dale, Imogen's intuition would have told her this. Equally, if she had needed to learn a lesson around rejection, she would have been compelled to ask Dale out. When she tried to get an intuitive answer about how this might go, she would have gotten a negative response, but she may have gone ahead with it anyway because it is such an emotionally-charged situation.

## Chapter 7 Review

Being sad or unhappy is not necessarily a "bad" thing. It is an indication of a lesson to be learned. If you believe that your natural state is happiness, then you could argue, and many do, that if you do not feel happy then you are expecting or wanting something from life that is not right for you just at this moment. This could be simply in the manner of your perspective. Perhaps you are sad about the ending of a relationship. But, perhaps it is actually that you have chosen to have been in denial about how bad the relationship was and the other person just realised it before you did and got out first, leaving you feeling rejected. It is the feeling of rejection that is causing you hurt, not the loss of a great asset from your life.

Just because you feel bad doesn't mean that being back in that relationship is the best thing for you. I believe that the best thing for you right now is whatever is happening in your life right now. That's not to say that you should sit by and let life happen around you, but try to work with and focus on what you do have to create what you want rather than moping over what you don't have. This is also where your intuition can help – by guiding you in which steps are most appropriate to take. If you keep coming up with negative or clouded intuitive feelings, try a different tack.

The great spiritual teacher, J. Krishnamurti, said that the key to his happiness was that he didn't mind what happened. Maybe when you reach this point, you will no longer need your intuition but, until then, it is an incredibly useful tool to have at your finger-tips!

# Chapter 8

# Visualisation

*"Dreaming, after all, is a form of planning."*

GLORIA STEINEM

Visualisation is a powerful tool for helping you to create *whatever* you want to create in your life regardless of whether it is a physical object or a set of circumstances. The real key, though, is in knowing what to put into your visualisation. By now, you're well on the way to knowing many of the things that your dream life includes, and this will naturally evolve as you learn and grow and experience more along the way to achieving it. There is always room for evolution and change. Life is a series of experiences which are all essential to your growth. So, your goal posts will be constantly moving. The movement may be hard to discern at times, but it will be there. Visualisation is a tool that can help you to both evolve your dreams and manifest your dreams.

### What Exactly Is Visualisation?

Visualisation is the process of creating a picture, or vision, of something in your mind, usually with the view to creating a clearer mental picture for yourself of something that you would like to have or create in your life. It's basically a focussed, intentional daydream. What you focus on could be something as simple as an apple. Many people use this as a meditation technique. The idea is that by focussing on something simple, like an apple, your conscious mind is kept occupied without having to do too much work, allowing your subconscious mind to push some ideas out in a way that you will notice them because your conscious mind isn't blocking them; it's busy doing something else.

Unless you are actually meditating or stranded in the desert with no food, visualising an apple is probably not going to excite you too much. What you want to be visualising are things that are relevant to your dream life. In actual fact, all things in existence have been visualised prior to their existence – otherwise, they would not and could not exist. They may not have been visualised by you, but, rather, by the person who designed them, say, in the case of a dress or a car. But, then again, many of the things in your life may have been previously visualised by you, just not consciously and with no particular focus or clarity.

For example, unless you had really strong ideas in your teens of what you thought you would be working as in your twenties, the strongest impressions would most likely have been the jobs of those closest to you, such as your parents. If your mother worked in an office or your father was a labourer, it is highly likely that you ended up doing one of these things as well, unless you had a pretty clear and focussed goal, perhaps encouraged by your parents, of doing something else.

## How do the Conscious and Subconscious Minds Work?

A subconscious visualisation is the result of subconscious expectations and happens without any effort from you. You can think of it as just an expectation you have because of the environment you grew up in, say, and it has never occurred to you to question it. By subconsciously visualising a particular outcome, say, of where you will work when you grow up, you make it more likely to come to fruition because you won't be considering other possibilities. Let's explore this a little further.

We previously talked about how much information you are bombarded with every second of the day and that your conscious mind only registers a small fraction of this information. Your subconscious mind, however, picks up everything. When you have an expectation, either consciously or subconsciously, your subconscious mind looks for opportunities that it knows will lead to having those things actually in your life, in the same way that you do consciously when, say, you're looking for a particular kind of dress or car.

You can think of the subconscious mind as your personal servant. Its job is to serve you and deliver to you things that you desire. Its only way of knowing what you desire is by taking note (creating and strengthening memories and links in your brain – see below) of what you draw its attention to through all of your physical senses and your emotions. However, it doesn't discriminate in terms of positive and negative; it bases its decision on volume and intensity. Those experiences that you have the most often, or that are the most emotionally intense, are the ones it will take the most notice of and, therefore, more diligently pursue opportunities for creating more of for you.

So how does this work in physical terms? We know that the brain builds up memory whereby new actions that you take, facts that you learn, or places that you visit are stored by creating new neural pathways. The more often you repeat an action, remember or use a fact, or visit a place, the stronger the neural pathway for the memory of it gets. Equally, a neural pathway will become weaker if the corresponding experience is not continually repeated. Pathways need to be maintained to remain strong. Your mind is, for our purposes here, the network of memories created by this process, along with the functionality of using these memories effectively for you.

So, it is useful to think of the conscious mind as consisting of a very small set of the strongest and most recent memories – those experiences that have happened most often or have been of the highest intensity, such as a traumatic event or a happily exciting one. Then the subconscious mind is all the rest. It has much more breadth and depth than the conscious mind as it has access to so many more experience types. With this analogy, there is not a hard and fast line between the conscious and subconscious minds; it is more of a gradual shift.

In this way, your subconscious mind also effectively acts as a constantly-evolving filter. It can most quickly recognise, or identify with, information that is similar to what it has gotten the most of in the past. Information that it only receives occasionally is ignored - or filtered out. Such information will register slightly, and may strengthen the corresponding neural pathway, but will quickly be overwhelmed by any incoming information corresponding to the stronger neural pathways.

So, if you are used to looking for what makes you happy in a situation, you will have strong neural pathways corresponding to being happy and to those things that make you happy. These will serve as a strong foundation for looking on the bright side of life, even in situations where others might find it difficult to consider that there even is a bright side. Equally, someone who is used to looking for the sad things in every situation will look at the same events as you but will experience them completely differently because their subconscious mind has developed a differently-shaped or tuned filter.

So, I hear you asking, why don't you look for opportunities consciously? Well, you do that as well. It's just that your subconscious mind has access to the whole picture of your past experiences whereas your conscious mind only accesses the tip of the iceberg, so to speak. Your subconscious mind is looking for what you really believe you can have, from its past conditioning, and not necessarily what you consciously think you want because of something you saw on television yesterday.

For example, if you say you want to be a rock star and write your own songs and sing on the world's biggest stages, you will consciously look for opportunities to sing and showcase your song writing abilities. But, if you've been told all of your life that you'll never amount to anything and it's too hard to be a successful singer, your subconscious mind will be looking for ways to make *that* true, instead, because those will actually be the strongest neural pathways in your brain with respect to this situation.

In this way, your subconscious may sabotage you so that you constantly procrastinate and never quite get a song finished. Or it might make sure you have a sore throat on the day you had agreed to meet with a talent scout. The way to overcome this is to start becoming aware of how your subconscious mind sabotages you or, if you can't identify any ways, simply start using your conscious mind to focus on the positive things in every situation and your subconscious will start to follow suit as those neural pathways get stronger. To see how this could work in your life, let's look at an example of how the subconscious mind can lead you in a direction in which you didn't necessarily consciously think you wanted to go.

## Anneliese's Story

Anneliese grew up in a typical middle-class suburb. Her mother was a primary school teacher and her father worked in an office as a clerk. Her aunt was also a teacher. From a very young age, Anneliese, would hear stories of teaching in a classroom from her mother and aunt and met many of her mother's, almost exclusively female, colleagues. She was often asked if she was going to be a teacher like her mum. She played "schools" with her dolls and her friends.

At the age of eight, she started ballet lessons which she really enjoyed and was quite good at. She may not have had the talent to be a prima ballerina in a national ballet company, but she was good enough that she began to get the idea that it might be nice to have her own ballet school when she grew up. Unfortunately, her parents weren't particularly encouraging. They were quite conservative and thought that opening a ballet school was quite risky. Neither of them knew anything about running a business.

They had both always been employees and liked the comfort of their pay being reliably deposited into their bank account every fortnight. The call for school teachers was always very high, it was very secure and, they pointed out to Anneliese, she had always loved playing schools with her dolls and friends as a young child. Teaching was a very nice profession for a young woman, especially if she was going to have a family. She could just work school hours! (I would like to just note here, that I have never met a school teacher who just worked school hours, unless they were part-time. My school teacher friends are the hardest working people I know!) Anneliese agreed, she did like playing school teacher, but she still kept in mind the idea that she'd like to open her own ballet school one day.

She continued with her ballet lessons right through until she finished high school. Then she had to decide what to do next. Even though she still liked the idea of having her own ballet school, she had imbibed her parents' strong need for security. After all, it had been drummed into her from a very young age. And she had believed their stories about the insecurity of having her own ballet school, so she thought she would just study a teaching degree to give her "something to fall back on". When she finished her teaching degree, she thought she should work for a year or two, just to get some experience under her belt and save some money with which to start her ballet school. Then she met and married a lovely man, and they started a family. Staying in teaching was good because they had a great maternity leave scheme and she could easily work part-time.

She forgot about the ballet school until she was 32, when she met up with a friend from high school and they started reminiscing. Her friend remembered Anneliese's desire to own her own ballet school. Anneliese was taken by surprise, initially, but said to her friend, "Oh yes, but I wouldn't know how to run a business anyway and it's not very secure, not while we have young children." Who does that sound like? That's right – her parents!

There is nothing right or wrong about what Anneliese did. She didn't love teaching, but she didn't hate it, either. She was quite happy with her family and the flexibility of working as a teacher. However, she never really stretched herself. She did what was expected of her by her family and herself because being a teacher and needing that strong security was drummed into her from a very young age. And, she never got to the point of really visualising herself owning and running a ballet school, at least not in a focussed way. So, her subconscious filter had been shaped to allow through thoughts, ideas, and information around "I am a teacher" and "I need security" and to filter out any "I own a ballet school" information.

Anneliese's life path is not so surprising, given the home environment that she grew up in. This is not a criticism of her parents. Their subconscious filters had also been shaped from a very young age and the information presented to them clearly also did not include much around owning their own business. They wanted the best for their daughter and security was very important to them, and it was therefore very important to them that Anneliese also had security. She was then also drawn to friends who had similar values. She wouldn't have understood or really been able to connect with anyone with much of an entrepreneurial mindset. Her ballet teacher could possibly have taken her aside and mentored her, perhaps into taking over her own school. However, Anneliese wouldn't have behaved in a way that would have led her teacher to consider this as a possibility because her subconscious filter was shaped in such a way that didn't really allow for this kind of behaviour.

There are a couple of ways in which Anneliese's attitude could change. Something could happen to snap her out of this way of thinking or else she could be exposed over time to different kinds of thinking. Something that could change her thinking in a snap might be the sudden death of a close friend, the breakdown of her marriage, or a scare for herself with a potentially terminal illness. Somehow such events often give us a wake-up call. Such an event, through its intensity, would create an immediate strong neural path in the brain, significantly changing the shape of the subconscious mind filter.

Such a traumatic event has led many people to live much more fulfilling lives afterwards because they are forced to question what is really important to them. They change their lives in terms of becoming more adventurous, not caring so much what others think, living for today and doing what they love instead of wasting time doing what others expect, that they don't love.

Another possibility would be if she found herself being surrounded by one or more people who are doing what they love, and show it, so that she was being constantly bombarded with their ideas that are different from her own. This would start building up those subconscious pathways, changing the shape of her filter to allow more of those kinds of ideas through. These could be parents of children in her classes, for example, or friends of her husband's. Or she could watch an episode of an inspirational program, like Oprah, that captures her imagination.

## *Why is Visualisation Important?*

We've covered the mechanics of how the conscious and subconscious minds are related and how they work. We've talked about how the brain establishes, builds and maintains neural pathways with every experience you have. Let's have a closer look at what constitutes an *experience*. Your body registers an experience based on external stimuli such as tastes, sounds, sights and smells. The registering of such experiences can evoke particular emotions such as happiness, sadness, or even curiosity.

What about *internal* stimuli? There are plenty of these, such as hunger pangs or the urge to sneeze, for example. These are automatic responses of your body. They are triggered unconsciously and you will never have – nor want! – conscious control over them, as they are securely programmed in to make sure your body functions as it should, without you having to think about it. But, what we're particularly interested in here is another type of internal stimuli – your thoughts.

It has been shown that the brain responds in exactly the same way whether you are imagining something happening or it is actually happening. That is, if you are thinking about carrying out a particular task, your brain creates or strengthens neural pathways in exactly the same way as if you were actually physically carrying out that task. Denis Waitley talks about how this theory has been tested on athletes and how it has been shown that when a sprinter, for example, visualises themselves running the 100m sprint from start to finish, the same nerve impulses are fired in their brains as if they were actually using the required muscles and running the race.

What an incredibly powerful concept! This means that you can use your imagination to visualise something and actually be building up the neural pathways for that experience, increasing its visibility to your subconscious mind. So, you can train your brain to respond in a certain way to a certain situation by just *imagining* it.

## More Helpful Hints for Finding Your Passion

As we have alluded to previously, one of the most difficult things about creating your dream life is actually working out what it looks like. The whole idea can seem so overwhelming that it can seem easier to give up before you even start. If you are in this situation, that you have so many ideas that you don't know where to start, the trick is to just choose one and start with that. You could write down all of the ideas you have and then compare and rank them all against each other until you have decided on one that you favour above all others. Or else, you could write down all of the things you think you might want on separate pieces of paper, put the pieces of paper into a container, shake it up a bit, and choose one. This is the one that you'll start with.

If you're not sure of anything that you want in your life, I suggest you go back to *Pause for Thought #9* and *Pause for Thought #10* and either do them again or read over what you have written, and also try some meditation for a week or two to let some ideas bubble up until you come across one that really excites you. Do also try to see if your subconscious is sabotaging you with respect to this because I know that you do really know what you want, but you're scared (consciously or subconsciously) of the consequences if you achieved it.

One way of helping to find something that you would passionately like to have in your life is to take a blank sheet of paper and write at the top of it "If money was no object, time was no object, I knew I couldn't fail and there were no other obstacles, what I would love to have in my life is...". The last part could also be something like "...what I would love to do is..." or "...what I would love to spend most of my time doing is..." Choose a phrase that works for you. In fact, the phrase that you choose is a good indication of the kinds of things you might like to have in your life. Then start writing down whatever answers come into your head, with a new line for each new idea.

To help you along a bit more if you're still struggling, most people, when truly provided with a choice, say through financial freedom, choose to do something creative (this doesn't have to be artistic – engineering, for example, is also a creative pursuit) and/or choose to do something that will be of service to others. I had lunch with a friend recently, who is now living her passion of exploring tertiary education, its presentation, delivery, and assessment. She made the comment that she could see herself travelling the world teaching people about what she thought she would find out through her research.

It struck me, particularly as I had also envisaged myself travelling the world talking to people about what I have discovered in the world of personal development, that perhaps that was a good indicator of your passion. When you think you'd love to tell others about a particular subject, because you are sure they'll find it as incredibly fascinating and useful as you do, that's exactly the subject you should be spending your time on!

*Pause for Thought #13: Creating Your Visualisation for Your Dream Life*

If you're still really stuck at this point, and you've done the values and obituary exercises and followed all of the suggestions above, it is almost certainly through subconscious sabotage, I suggest you just do the visualisation exercise we're about to talk about, for something you love to eat, like chocolate (that's certainly something I love to eat!), winning a gold medal at the Olympics (maybe the 100m sprint or gymnastics), or else singing in front of a huge, adoring audience in a large stadium.

### *Preparation*

Okay, so we're going to assume now that you have something that you really want in your life that you can focus on for your visualisation. Visualisation is best done by a combination of sitting and closing your eyes and having a pen and paper to write down your thoughts. Writing down your thoughts will be a combination of what you just created in your visualisation and just letting your thoughts flow in a steady stream to help to evolve an effective picture.

### *Getting Comfortable*

I suggest you start by sitting yourself in a comfortable position – not too comfortable, though, as you don't want to fall asleep! The essence of your visualisation will, obviously, depend on the nature of what it is that you're visualising. It is unlikely that you'll come up with a picture that you're perfectly happy with straight away. You will need to create it by becoming aware of what your subconscious chose to put in there initially, with what you consciously think would be better, by adding to it and replacing less ideal details with better ones until you're satisfied with it. Don't forget, you're still fighting against what your subconscious is most familiar with, so it will not provide you with the most effective picture without some intervention!

### Exploring Your Visualisation

Okay, so you should now have your initial picture. I want you to now explore your picture in as much detail as you can. You should notice your feelings, the people around you, what you are saying to them, how you are treating them, what they are saying to you, how they are treating you, the objects around you, their textures and colours, any smells or sounds. Take particular note of yourself in this picture – what are you wearing, how is your hair styled, are you standing or sitting, and so on. Many things you will not be aware of until you start asking yourself these questions.

### Getting It Down On Paper

Some things will appear to you immediately but others you will find difficult to picture. For the more difficult or vague things you are free to create what you think should be there to make the scene seem right. Once you have a picture that you are happy with, it would be a good idea to write down all of the ideas that you have. I suggest pen and paper rather than an electronic device because you may wish to include some quick sketches to illustrate your idea, and this is still generally easier to do on paper.

The first time you attempt your visualisation will probably take the longest. On subsequent occasions, you may not need to write down quite as much. However, it will be evolving as your subconscious becomes attuned to it and starts adding or allowing in new details, which may not have come through the first few times. This will become more fun as you relax into it and learn to let yourself go. As you start exploring your visualisation you will come up with new ideas and begin to see more of what is possible, coming up with scenarios you may not have let yourself contemplate in the past.

There is no right or wrong amount of time to spend on visualising. Even five minutes might be enough. Do make it regular, though; once a day would be great. More if you can fit it in. The first few times, at least, it is a good idea to look at what you have written down in your previous sessions to get you back into it quickly. Each time you do it, you are strengthening the neural pathways in your brain and training your subconscious to look out for opportunities to help you to realise the picture in your visualisation. This brings us to how you actually achieve the picture in your visualisation, in real life.

## Taking Action or Creating Your Dream Life in Real Life

Visualising your dream life or dream scenario is a powerful tool but it is not enough all by itself to cause it to come to fruition. At some point, you obviously have to actually take some action, and appropriate action at that. Once you get used to the process of visualisation and you have a compelling scenario worked out for yourself, you will then need to start focussing on how you're going to get there. While your subconscious mind will be working on this to some degree, it will work much more effectively if your conscious mind is also working on it. The experiences and stimuli that your conscious mind is aware of are most likely to form stronger neural pathways than those that go straight through to the subconscious mind.

So, here is one of the most effective ways I have found for working out what action to take. It is identical to the suggestion above about what to do when you're really, really stuck on what you should be visualising. That is, take a piece of paper (again you can do this electronically, but I find using a pen and paper to be more effective) and at the top write "Action steps for achieving my visualised goal of X" where you would replace "X" with a description of the scenario or desirable thing you have been focussing on in your visualisations. Now, just let the ideas flow out onto the page. Just write down whatever comes into your mind. At first the ideas may be very much at a surface level or, perhaps, shallow. They may even be nonsensical. But, as you get more of them out of your brain and onto the paper, it seems to clear room in your brain to allow the more thoughtful and useful ideas to flow out.

Depending on the size of your visualised goal, you may want to break it down into smaller chunks first. Identify what the first goal might be on the way to the full visualised goal and carry out the writing process for just that first step. Once you have written as many ideas as you can think of and have come up with some actions that you believe would be effective in helping you to reach your first goal, you should create a plan for carrying out those actions. If one of the action steps in your plan is really obvious, like simply making a phone call, hop to it. Immediately! Now you can move onto the next action step.

Note that this whole process is not a static one. Even though you may have come up with a list of steps to reach your final goal, this list could well change as you achieve your sub-goals along the way. You may find that taking particular actions will achieve more or possibly less than you had originally anticipated. They may throw up obstacles which you hadn't considered.

The most important thing, though, is DON'T PANIC, as the cover of *The Hitchhikers Guide to the Galaxy* says, and don't give up. When you come up against an unforeseen obstacle, you just need to go through the same process to come up with an action plan for getting around, through, over or under it. And, if a particular action or sequence of actions happens to achieve more than you had anticipated, that's great! It may even help you to realise that you can create and achieve an even more ambitious vision than you had originally come up with.

## Chapter 8 Review

Visualisation is a powerful tool for many reasons. The best thing about it is that when you visualise a situation, and really get into the feeling of it – the smells, the sounds, what your body is doing – your brain doesn't know the difference between thinking about it and actually doing it. So you can train your brain to know what it's like to be *anything you can dream of*! You will actually be creating neural pathways in your brain for whatever experience you like, just by thinking about it. The more often you visualise a particular situation or experience, the more familiar it will be to you and the more natural it will seem to you to take the steps required to make it happen in real life, so the more likely you will be to do just that.

Further, the more you focus on a situation, through visualisation, the more you can hone it to smooth out the kinks. As you become more and more familiar with your visualised scenario, you'll become clearer on which parts you want to keep and which parts you want to change. You can experiment without taking a step out the door, or even lifting a finger. And by doing this enough, you may be able to avoid many mistakes in real life because you will already have anticipated them in your visualisation and come up with great alternatives.

The trick is to get a balance. Obviously you've got to actually get out there and take some real, physical action at some point, but doing some visualisation will give you a much greater chance of taking the right action that will give you the results you're looking for.

# Chapter 9

# Making The Transition

*"People often say motivation doesn't last. Neither does bathing—that's why we recommend it daily."*

ZIG ZIGLAR

It's great having an idea of what you want your life to look like. You may even have an idea of what the first couple of steps are that you need to take. On paper, this seems fairly straight forward. In reality, though, it can be a different story. If you make changes in your life, it is likely to affect other people. Have you included them in your plans? And how are they going to react to your vision for a new life? And then there's your own inner self that has got you to where you are now and may be a bit miffed that you want to change things when it is quite comfortable with how things are, thank you very much. And it is going to be particularly influential when you come up against obstacles and things get tough. In this chapter we're going to look at the kinds of things that are most likely to hold you back and how you can overcome them to keep you on the road to your fabulous, passion-filled new life.

## *What You Don't Know That You Expect*

You have a dream of a different life, an exciting new life. After reading the previous chapter, you've got a vision of how you want it to look. Not only is this important, it is essential. If you don't know where you're going, you'll arrive somewhere else, as they say. Unfortunately, though, as your vision is most likely quite a long way from where your life currently is, it may be that your subconscious thoughts have not yet caught up with your vision.

One of the first things we talked about in this book is how influenced you are by where and how you grew up, and who with, and how this information seeps into your subconscious, affecting how you live your life. This is pretty deep-seated stuff and it is wedged in pretty tightly. The worst thing about it is that we are mostly unaware of it. So, the danger is that, even if you consciously want to change how your life looks, your subconscious mind is almost certainly still attached to and thinking in the old ways.

## Zac's Story

Zac was working as an accountant but he dreamed of becoming a comedian. He had been writing some jokes and routines after work and on the weekends, but he knew that for his comedy career to take off, he really needed to get himself in front of an audience. Unfortunately, as he was growing up, he was told many times that children are seen and not heard; whenever adults were invited to the house for dinner parties, which was often, he and his sister were sent off to bed early; and often when the current affairs programs were on the television after family dinners, he was allowed to remain in the room, but had to keep quiet while his parents watched.

His parents weren't purposely trying to make Zac feel like he should be hidden away. They were simply passing on behaviours they had seen from their parents and were doing what they thought was right. They spent time with their children and took them to play sports and so on, but when they had guests, they wanted to be able to have what they called "adult time" without the children interrupting. Finally, when he was young, he had been a bit of a clown, but he had had a particularly strict teacher in grade three who had told him to be quiet, or sent him to stand outside every time he'd spoken just a bit too loudly.

All of these experiences added up so that Zac had an underlying sense that he was not to make a spectacle of himself, that he should not and could not "put himself out there". That is, he was effectively *programmed*, like a computer, to feel this way. His subconscious expectations were that he shouldn't go out in front of people because he shouldn't be heard (which is why he chose an occupation like accountancy in the first place – it can be easy to keep to yourself or, at least, not have to express opinions when you do deal with people, as most of what accountants deal with is objective rather than subjective.)

So, he was finding it very difficult to make himself actually look for places where he could present his comedy routines, let alone actually call any of them. He always seemed to manage to come up with an excuse – it's too late, I'll do it in the morning; or I've got too much to do today, I can do it tomorrow, or next week, and so on. Or else, in the time that he had scheduled for it, something else came up, like he suddenly got a migraine and had to go to bed to sleep it off.

## *Ferreting Out Your Subconscious Expectations*

If you know what you want to do, but find yourself making excuses, or sabotaging yourself, like Zac, it is highly likely that you also have some underlying, subconscious fears or beliefs, that are holding you back. The reality is that, like everyone else, you will have been affected by events or experiences in your early childhood. You will have been affected to a lesser or greater extent by these experiences, depending on how intense they were, how frequent they were and how the rest of your life has been. But don't despair! There is a way to get past this kind of programming.

Possibly the most important part of such programming, rather than the experience itself, is the decision you made about yourself as a result of the events or experiences that led to this programming. Becoming aware of that decision is the key to moving forward. For example, Zac may have made the decision that, because he shouldn't be seen, he wasn't a worthy person and, therefore, he didn't deserve to be listened to because he had nothing worth saying. This was quite an attitude to overcome if he wanted to become a comedian.

The decision you made as a small child (and there could have been many, affecting various parts of your life now), that is stopping you from changing what you do every day (your job versus your passion), is what your subconscious has held onto for all of these years to keep you safe in that area of your life. Once little Zac made the decision that he didn't deserve to be listened to because he had nothing worth saying, his subconscious mind took it on board and used it as a rule. The rule was: "Zac has nothing worthwhile to say. Ever. If he does try to express an opinion he will be ostracised and feel foolish and humiliated. And this must be avoided at all costs."

So, to keep Zac safe from feeling foolish and humiliated, his subconscious mind made sure over the years that he didn't put himself into a position for this to happen. Whenever Zac ventured to express an opinion or speak out, his subconscious whispered to him, "No, you can't do that, because you don't have anything worthwhile to say and you'll be laughed at and humiliated.", which Zac would have "heard" as a knot in his stomach and a sense of dread or even deep sadness. You could also think of this as a form of resistance, which we discussed in the case of Sunita, earlier. When you come across resistance, it is your subconscious giving you a warning that you are in danger of breaking a rule you made long ago (and hold in its own little neural memory pocket) that it has endeavoured to abide by to keep you safe.

It can make an enormous difference in your life if you can accept that you are fully responsible for what is currently in your life because it is a result of the decisions you made about yourself and what you deserve, as a small child. While your subconscious mind made those decisions in your best interests at the time, many of those decisions are most likely not serving you particularly well at all at this stage in your life and now you have an opportunity to discard them. If you are fully responsible for what is in your life right now, then that means that you can change it, if you really want to.

Understanding or accepting this is helpful in getting to the bottom of the decisions the little you made that are stopping the adult you from moving forward. By understanding and accepting that these are decisions that *you* made, it takes away any sense of blame from anyone else, as well as any underlying sense of resentment towards them. If you take the responsibility onto yourself, it makes it easier for you (and your subconscious mind) to accept that you can actually do something about it. You can feel in control of your life. Of course the tricky bit can be working out exactly what those subconscious decisions were.

### *Pause for Thought #14: Subconscious Decisions About Yourself*

The questions in this *Pause for Thought* are designed to help you to unearth the early decisions you made about yourself. At the top of a shiny, new sheet of paper, write the question that you are seeking an answer to that has to do with you being stuck. For example, Zac might write, "Why am I not allowing myself to be a comedian?" or simply, "Why am I not a comedian?" Some other examples you could try (or variations of them) include:

- Why am I stuck in a job I hate?
- Why don't I leave this job that I hate?

- Why don't I study (x)?
- Why am I not a (x)?
- Why don't I know what my passion is?

Write your question in the present tense. If it's in the past tense, it signals to your subconscious that you only think you could have been/done that thing in the past and you don't really intend to pursue it now. By putting it that way you will have put another barrier in your way because, if it's in the past, your subconscious doesn't have to worry about it and won't be inclined to give you a real answer.

Now, write down each answer that comes into your head, even if they don't appear to make sense initially. This works by clearing out the fluff (nonsense answers) that has been blocking the real reasons and now giving your subconscious mind the space to delve deeply and reveal the real reasons. Rather than saying to yourself, "That's nonsense!" to any nonsense answers that come out, just acknowledge them, without judgement (maybe say to yourself, "Thank you, that's interesting."), and move on to the next answer, until they start making more sense.

You have to be a bit accommodating to your subconscious mind, humour it, so that it will feel inclined or comfortable enough to reveal the truth to you. Remember, it has been hiding this stuff for a very long time. It may need some coaxing. Sooner or later, you will come to an answer that makes you go "Aha!" (or something like that). This will give you a clue as to the decisions you made about yourself, that are stopping you from living your passions. You may need several sessions before you get to any "Aha!" answers, depending on how dependent your subconscious mind is on the identity it has built for you around these decisions. The more dependent it is, the harder it is going to find it to give them up.

### *Why is Your Old Thinking So Persistent?*

Once you have discovered what has been holding you back, you'll need a way to integrate your new thinking and maintain it. Remember you have been operating in this other way for many, many years and, even though you're now aware of what has been holding you back, it will take some time to establish a new way of thinking, particularly because you are most likely still in the environment in which you have been living out the old thinking. If you suddenly change your thinking and attitude, you are most likely to come up against resistance from the people around you. People seldom like change unless they feel they have some control over it or unless they can at least see obvious benefits to themselves. Even if you think the changes you are making are positive, it may take others some time to catch up with you, if they ever do. We will discuss what to do about this in Chapter 12.

So let's talk about your environment and its influence on you and how you can counter it. Remember how we talked about how the bulk of our ideas were instilled in us as little people and, just above, about the decisions you made about yourself that have ruled your life ever since. To change your ideas and expectations, you need to acquire – and integrate – some new ideas.

One of the biggest barriers that we face in making a change is recognising that we are filled with biases and prejudices about how the world works. To illustrate with a visual example, consider a gender-neutral person, as in Figure 3. Let's call this person a common gender-neutral name, Sam. Sam thinks that everyday life is neutral; that the messages s/he gets are just the way things are. What Sam doesn't realise is that s/he has been filled up with the grey sludge of the everyday messages that s/he has chosen to be bombarded with. That's right – *chosen*.

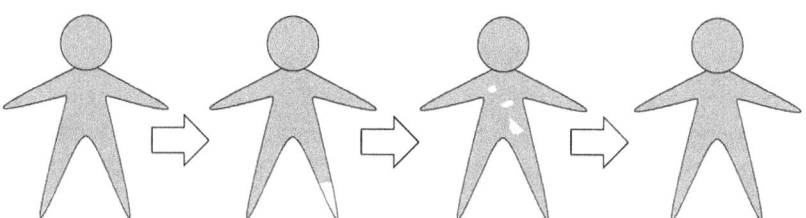

Figure 3: We get filled with the grey sludge of the messages we are being bombarded with every day. Sometimes we get new bright ideas but they disperse and disappear quickly if they're not constantly replenished.

Most of us tend to live within our comfort zones. This includes the friends we have, the places we work, the things we watch on television, the books we read, and even the websites we frequent. We hang around with people who have similar backgrounds, ideas and attitudes to life that we have. (If they are different – such as having different political or religious/spiritual views, we tend to avoid those topics.) We may watch a small number of particular television programs on a regular basis. They may be different from each other but our regular watching ensures that we are getting the same small group of ideas reinforced over and over again. Even the newspaper articles in a particular newspaper are pretty much identical from day to day. Just the names and places will have changed.

So, let's get back to Sam. Let's imagine that the information that Sam is being bombarded with enters at her/his big toe on her/his left foot, circulates around her/his body and then finally seeps out at the top of her/his head. Sam is all grey because s/he is only taking in the grey messages in her/his comfort zone. Then one day, Sam is invited along to a seminar by a friend. The seminar could be on wealth creation or personal development, say. The ideas at this seminar are new and exciting; different from anything Sam has really been exposed to previously. These are *bright* ideas! Bright ideas start to seep in through Sam's left big toe and, by the end of the weekend seminar, have filled her/him up to the left knee, forcing out some of the grey.

Unfortunately, though, Sam goes home on Sunday night to her/his "normal" life where s/he is again bombarded by the grey sludge messages. So, by about Wednesday the bright has been displaced by the new grey seeping in through Sam's big toe. The bright is dispersing and integrating with the grey, so its strength and power of influence over Sam's thinking is quickly dissipating. By the following weekend, the bright has all seeped out and Sam is full of the grey sludge again!

## Making Your New Thinking Stick

So, how can Sam, and you, make the changes in ideas, attitude and expectations stick? The key is *persistence*. Just going to one seminar or reading one book is unlikely to give you lasting change. There is a useful analogy, used as the quote of this chapter, by Zig Ziglar, which points out that we bathe every day because we get dirty every day, and so it is with motivation. Similarly, because we get newly "dirtied" with the grey sludge every day, we need to "bathe" in the new bright ideas every day.

There are many options available to us for such bathing. We can read books, listen to audio, watch videos, attend seminars, get a life coach or mentor, or any combination of these. The great thing is that all of these options, including the life coach/mentor, have both physical (or in-person) options and online options. For example, I coach many of my clients over Skype. This enables me to have clients from all over the world, to coach clients wherever they happen to be in the world and, for those in the same city, saves us both precious time in travel.

These options do, however, have varying levels of general effectiveness, due to their particular modes of learning and interaction. The first three options are pretty much individual. You generally read a book, listen to audio (say, in the car on the way to work or during your daily exercise) and watch videos by yourself. The same issue of relative isolation occurs if you choose to "attend" online seminars such as teleseminars and webinars, even if they are live.

Attending live seminars where you are physically in the same room as the presenter(s) and the other participants is a step up from this. You meet many like-minded people who are also interested in changing themselves to achieve a more fulfilling life. If you're diligent, one of the most effective ways of continuing to grow from and integrate the material from such a seminar is to keep in touch with one or more of the people you meet at such events. In this way, you can support and encourage each other over the coming months and years as you transition to your new life. Talking to your new friends can help to keep you filling up with the bright ideas and keep the grey sludge at bay.

I have met many of my best friends at such seminars and have found them to be an invaluable source of encouragement and information. More often than not, because they are people who are also seeking change, they have come across and utilised many ideas that I have not. They can be a great resource. Further, when you achieve your goals and milestones, these people will be among your greatest supporters. They will certainly help you to celebrate, even if it is from a distance. This can be a great boost when you find that your family and "old" friends do not quite understand the new you with your new bright ideas.

## *When Your Family and Friends Don't Get the New You*

Generally, when the topic of comfort zones is discussed, it is put in terms of "expanding". The saying goes that once you expand your comfort zone, it can never contract back to what it was. I see it as working a little differently from this. I think that picturing your comfort zone as being represented by a colour is more apt as, having changed the colour of your comfort zone, say from grey towards bright, means that it is likely that you will no longer feel comfortable with the ideas and attitudes from your old, grey, comfort zone.

For example, if you've lived away from your parents' home for some years, how often have you cringed, when you go back to visit, when you find that they're having the same conversations and complaining about the same things, in the same way, that they did when you were a child or a teenager? You have experienced some different things in the world and your comfort zone has changed, at least slightly, from your parents' – particularly if you have moved to a different city, country, or culture.

This can be another challenge of wanting to change, which many people find very difficult to overcome, even more difficult than escaping the grey sludge. Your family and friends may actively resist the changes you make. We all tend to stick within our comfort zones, unless forced out, for example, by a personal tragedy. Your family and friends are also sticking within their comfort zones. Up until now, your comfort zones have largely harmonised.

In fact, you can almost think of society as being made up of many groups with slightly different comfort zone types and, therefore, sludge colours. So, as you start to permanently take on more and brighter ideas, your comfort zone will be changing and may start to clash with the comfort zones of your family and friends. You can try to bring them along with you but, in most cases, this won't be possible – they will need to find their own way out of the sludge when they are ready. The reality is that you may need to change who you hang out with.

You don't have to ditch all of your friends the day after your first seminar with bright ideas. What is more likely to happen is that you may naturally start to drift away from some of them as your ideas expand and you find that you no longer enjoy spending time with them as much. The reality is that their comfort zones may not harmonise with yours because your comfort zone is no longer grey, it is becoming brighter. Don't assume that you'll now have no friends, though. You will simply be making new friends. You will be finding friends who fit in with your new way of thinking, your new, more brightly coloured comfort zone.

Moving away from your family, metaphorically speaking, can be more of a challenge. (Here, I am referring to your birth family, not your marital family, if that applies to you.) How much of an issue this is in moving forward will depend on how supportive they are of you. It may be that you simply have to limit the topics of your conversations or the number of conversations and visits you have with them. You could also have a supportive person, maybe one of your new bright friends, on notice that you'll need to debrief with them after a family visit.

## Financial Freedom

One more thing that can help you to transition from your current life to your dream life is having your finances on track for financial freedom or, at least, financial independence. One of the big issues that I see that stops people from following their dreams is the issue of financial security. In our society, we have managed to couple our financial security with what we do every day. As Alan Watts says in his fabulous short video, "What if Money Didn't Matter?", which has been doing the social media rounds: "You'll be doing things you don't like doing in order to go on living, that is to go on doing the things you don't like doing."

That is, once we have a job, even if we don't like it, we tend to get used to having that amount of money very quickly and our lifestyle matches or, more often with our current ease of access to credit, exceeds our income. So we feel trapped into staying in this job, whether we like it or not, in order to afford all of the expenses we have chosen to have in our lives (notice I have again purposely used the word *chosen*). This doesn't allow for the mental space to even consider doing something else, even if it is something that we love. And this is often because we assume that we couldn't spend all of our time doing what we love because it wouldn't make us enough money; but, enough money for what?

In our world of amassing material possession, where does one stop? If you do get to be the overwhelmingly rich with several houses, luxurious swimming pools, designer clothes, shoes and jewels, helicopters, private jets and sports cars, then what? What will having all of those material possessions do for you? What will it mean? What will you aim for next?

I suspect that you are thinking about philanthropic ventures. You may want to establish a hospital in a developing country or provide scholarships to university – or even school – for children from disadvantaged backgrounds. It tends to be these kinds of pursuits – where you feel like you're making a real contribution to the world – that really drive people to keep achieving. Regardless of where you think you'd put your money, if you had complete financial freedom, I hope this has started you thinking about what you are aiming for and why. And that is the absolute key – knowing why. In fact, you need to have a why before you can come up with an appropriate and clear what. There is nothing inherently wrong with amassing material possessions, it is the why that is the issue.

If we could separate our financial security from what we do every day, this would allow us to relax a little and step back to see the bigger picture of our lives. So, how do you separate the two? Admittedly, for most of us, this does require at least a few years of working and earning money based on what you do each day. The alternative is if you're particularly entrepreneurial and come up with a great idea that you can convince others to fund for you. However, let's assume that you're the typical person who has come through our education system which pushes the "go to school – get good marks – get a good job" regime.

Getting wealthy is actually remarkably simple, no matter what your income is, if you follow a few simple rules. The first is to pay yourself first. That is, of the money you get paid each week, set aside a certain amount for security and investing, preferably no less than 10% (otherwise it will take too long to build up to a useful amount). What you have left over is what you can spend. The next rule, then, is to spend less than you earn. Ridiculously simple, but so often not followed today because we have evolved a rampant credit culture. Borrowing money to accumulate assets is one thing, but borrowing money to buy everyday items does not make good financial sense. And, finally, invest the money you put aside under the first rule, for growth.

I would also recommend that you determine a monthly budget. Anything smaller or larger than this is either too small to allow you to see the bigger picture or else more difficult to keep track of. You will find that some months you have annual or quarterly bills due. It's easiest to manage your money if you can make the budget the same for every month. One way you can manage this is by arranging regular payments to be taken from your account for these quarterly and annual bills so that there is never a spike in your monthly costs. However, this may not always be possible. Another option is, when you have two or more large bills due in the same month, shift one of them to the previous month, and pay it early. This will effectively smooth out your monthly costs.

This is not a financial advice book, and I am not a qualified financial adviser, so I highly recommend that you find and see a good financial adviser. You want someone who actually cares about what you do. A good financial adviser does not work on commission, they get paid by actual services carried out – that is on the time they spend working out the best options for you. They will also explore your financial *and* life goals. I can also highly recommend a book called *The Richest Man in Babylon*, which has some great wealth wisdom written as parables set in ancient Babylon. It promotes the ideas written here and includes some great stories.

It doesn't matter if you are starting from scratch, or if you have a couple of investment properties and a share portfolio under your belt, you can start putting these principles into practice right now. This is not a get-rich-quick regime but it *is* a guaranteed get-rich over time scheme – if you follow the rules.

## *Chapter 9 Review*

Transitioning from your current way of life to a different one is not necessarily an easy path. It requires planning and preparation. Most of the preparation is mental preparation. You are in your current situation because of decades of thinking in a certain way and having that way of thinking constantly reinforced by doing the same things, being around the same people and going to the same places.

For most of us, making a big shift in our lives takes a lot of effort. But that's no reason why you shouldn't do it. Most things worth having take a lot of effort. To help you to keep pushing through, set yourself up financially and surround yourself with people who will support you and cheer you on. And keep bathing yourself in the new ideas that you want to live by so that they become second nature to you. You will have transformed before you know it.

# Chapter 10

# Developing A Business Plan

*"It does not do to leave a live dragon out of your calculations, if you live near him."*

J. R. R. TOLKIEN, The Hobbit

Once you've worked out your passion, or chosen one to focus on, it's likely that you'll want to start a business of some sort in order to pursue it in such a way that also makes you money – hopefully enough to support yourself so that you can keep doing it! It's certainly a good idea to see an accountant about this to get the right financial and legal structures in place. However, whether you do this or not, you need to be getting on with living your passion and, hopefully, making money out of it. To do this, you need to have customers or clients of some description. People need to know about you. You need to understand the market, and maybe look for opportunities for joint ventures, which can be a great way of learning and leveraging from someone else's experience.

This chapter is not meant to be the definitive business plan manual. There are plenty of good books, courses and other resources available for you to find out all of the details you'll need for your specific business. What this chapter is meant to be is a "starter pack". It is particularly for people who have never owned their own business and have possibly never even heard the term "business plan". This is very much a beginner's guide. We will go through the basics of what you will need to be thinking about to get your business off the ground and to move it forward in the direction that you want it to.

## Taking the Right Action

In the personal development world, many theories are declared around how your attitude and thoughts help to propel you forward in life. I believe that these theories are, indeed, true. What I have trouble with is when the speaker attempts to provide a scientific-sounding explanation to the theory which is, at best, vague; at worst, severely flawed. Now, they aren't being vague or flawed on purpose. It is almost certain that they are simply passing on what they were taught, in the way they were taught it. However, vague (and, certainly, flawed) explanations can really take away from the value of the idea. I find myself struggling with the reliability and truth of the explanation rather than just accepting the idea and using it, at least until I can come up with an explanation that is acceptable to me.

I am going to give an example from the movie, *The Secret*. I would like to firstly say, though, that I absolutely loved the movie and have watched it at least 100 times. Its simple message, that we create our world through what we think about, really captivated me. As an introduction to the basic idea of creating your world through what you think, it does its job really well. Now, in this movie, there is much talk of everything consisting of energy and this is absolutely true. I have no argument with that. There is also much mention of the word "vibration". Again, vibration is an essential component of energy, whether it is heat energy, sound energy or electrical energy. The idea is expressed that everything moves "into form, through form and back into form again". It all sounds very scientific. Except that it's not.

I think that what they were trying to say was that energy never gets destroyed. As it has been shown that, fundamentally, energy and matter are equivalent (think Einstein's $E=mc^2$ equation, where $E$ is energy, $m$ is mass or matter and $c$ is the speed of light), let's look at this statement involving energy and form in terms of matter, instead. Matter – or physical material – is something we're all familiar with and deal with every day, whereas energy is a far more nebulous concept.

So, let's take that expression and energy and form and consider it in terms of matter. Atoms are a fundamental component of matter and, nuclear explosions aside, are never destroyed. So, we can say that the atoms that were around when Julius Caesar was alive are still around – they just now exist in a different object (or form) than they did at that time. For example, a nitrogen atom that was, at one time, a part of the skin on Cleopatra's nose, may now be floating around in the atmosphere above Antarctica or be part of the tomato that will be in your salad tomorrow – from whence it may become a part of the skin on your nose!

In a similar vein, many explain the law of attraction as a simple matter of attuning your vibration to that which you seek (by thinking about it and visualising having it while in a truly positive state of mind – without any underlying doubts). This explanation actually does appeal to me but, as I am trying to keep this book as "down to Earth" and practical as possible, I would like to present, instead, a less esoteric explanation. As we focus on what we want, and get really clear on it, our subconscious is trained to look out for opportunities that lead us to that outcome. I think of it as causing our subconscious to work away at possible schemes for achieving what we want. So we find ourselves being drawn to situations, people and places that can help us achieve what we want as our subconscious does its work – by making us take notice when such things come into our experience.

I have had many examples in my own life where I put an idea "out there" and events conspired to turn that idea into reality with seemingly little conscious effort from me. For example, I decided that I wanted to leave my academic job at the beginning of the year. As an academic I was required to give six months' notice, to allow for teaching duties, so I had decided I would give notice at the end of June to be out by the end of the year. I had no idea how I was going to afford it. I had some long service and annual leave still owing but, looking back now, that probably wasn't going to be enough to give me the time I needed to transition to a completely new lifestyle.

However, in March, an email was sent to all university employees, implying that redundancies were a possibility. This had not happened for several years. I put up my hand to volunteer for a redundancy and was able to leave in August with a significant amount more than I had expected at the beginning of the year, and four and half months sooner that I had originally planned. I have many similar stories to this. And I will bet that you do, too. The key to it, though, was that I took action. I spoke to the right people to get the process in place – when I saw the appropriate opportunity (a potential payout) – and made sure that things were moving along when I hadn't heard anything for a while. And this is what you need to do to live your passion – keep taking action.

## How to Find Your Niche

One of the first things people will tell you when you are thinking of starting a business is that you have to have a niche. For some businesses and products, the niche is obvious. A teddy bear, for example, is likely to be targeted at the under-threes (or those who buy for the under-threes, like grandparents), unless it is a plush, collectible bear in which case it will be targeted at, well, bear collectors.

When I was first thinking about starting a coaching business, people kept asking me what my niche was. I found this idea quite daunting. Coaching was quite different from what I had done in the past, so how could I know what my niche was if I hadn't started yet and hadn't worked out what about it I really loved or was even good at? Finally, another coach reassuringly told me that they thought it was okay to practice for a while first to work out what my niche should be. This was such a relief and made a lot of sense.

If you are looking at something like coaching where you are dealing directly with people, you may want to hold off a bit on your niche as well, unless you're really confident of exactly who you want to help. One of the best ways to do this is to give free sessions for a few months. If you can find a few people to "practise" on, they will benefit from what you do know and you will benefit through gaining some confidence and working through where your strengths are and where your weaknesses are, and just what kinds of people with what kinds of problems, you enjoy working with. This is great knowledge to have.

And this goes for any new business idea. For example, if you're an artist, you may wish to cater to the corporate world, having your work displayed in office reception areas for greater exposure. There are different levels here, too. Do you want your work displayed in small local businesses or are you aiming for the head offices of the corporate giants? Or maybe you're content with the Sunday market crowd. The thing is, unless you're one of those rare people who has had a specific burning ambition that hasn't wavered since they were five, you will almost certainly need to give yourself some time to experiment with what feels right for you.

One way of at least narrowing your niche down fairly quickly is to brainstorm of all of the possible niches that you can think of for your passion. By all means use friends, family, the internet, and your favourite search engine to help you here, and don't forget the framework in Chapter 5. Often it can be hard to get out of your own way. You are limited in the ideas you will allow through because of your preconceptions and prejudices around what is reasonable. Find as many other places and people for ideas as you can.

When the focus isn't on you it can be much easier to be outlandish, or super-creative, in your ideas; so your friends may come up with more creative or inventive ideas for you than you would for yourself. If you won't be depending on the outcome, you'll be more prepared to see past your own, often unspoken or even unrecognised, prejudices around "what isn't realistic". You never know, some of your friends may be inspired to look at new possibilities for their own lives, too.

## Developing Your Networks

No matter what area your new business or career choice is in, networking is absolutely worth its weight in gold. You never know where the next great idea, inspiration, mentor, or just plain good friend is going to come from. If you haven't already been an active networker or if you need to establish a new network because your new pursuit is quite different from anything you've previously done, start looking for networking groups in your city. Okay, this is pretty obvious! What is not always obvious is what the most appropriate networking groups will be for you or, in fact, where they are. Even though the internet has been around for 20 or so years, now, things aren't always as easy to find as we would like. I have found that I have come across at least as many networking groups via word of mouth as I have through Google.

Like your niche, finding the right networking groups for you is a matter of trial and error. And don't neglect online networking, such as LinkedIn and Facebook, as well as the many other more specific forums. I have met several great people through connecting via online forums and then meeting them in person, because one or the other of us found the other's profile interesting. In one way, meeting this way can be more time-efficient because you can search on particular keywords to find people with profiles that are likely to be of mutual benefit.

On the other hand, face-to-face networking allows you to meet many people at once and you can gauge straight away whether you "click" with each person; plus face-to-face conversations can allow for ideas to come up, as the conversation flows, that wouldn't so easily come up over an internet message exchange where only one of you has the proverbial floor at a time. So, it is worthwhile pursuing both on-line and in-person networking.

The next question, then, is what to do when you get to a networking event. To get the best out of any kind of networking, it is best if you can have a plan or vision for what you want to get out of it and a plan for following up. Many people find networking quite nerve-wracking, especially if they're fairly new to it. So be assured, if you're nervous, other people will be too. The thing to realise is that everyone wants to be liked and to make a good impression. The biggest key to networking is remembering that it is about building relationships. And this is the thing that should be topmost in your mind when you go along to any networking event.

For your first few times with a particular group, then, you should be focussing on chatting to as many people as possible, and finding out about them and what they do. I would highly recommend taking particular note of the people that you felt a particular rapport with – you're creating a new life that you love, so you want to make sure you have people in it who enhance that vision. However, don't completely dismiss the ones that you don't have an immediate rapport with – if they're a bit out of sorts, you never know what's going on in their lives that may be affecting them or they may just be shy and take a few meetings to come out of their shell.

For the first few meetings your plan could be as simple as to meet as many people as possible. To help you to feel a bit more confident when you go in, have a few questions up your sleeve to ask, apart from the obvious "What do you do?" such as:

- How did you choose to get into the business you're in?
- What is the main service that you provide to help people?
- What makes your business special or unique, compared to others in the same area?
- What is your niche and how did you come to it?
- What is the most rewarding aspect of what you do?
- In an ideal world, what would your business look like?
- What's your biggest goal for the next 12 months?
- What do you see as the biggest challenge in your business over the next 12 months?

You can also use their answers to generate more questions, as appropriate. Also make sure that you have one or two things to say about what you do, or are planning to do. Don't be concerned about telling people that you're just starting out, although if you at least had the beginnings of a vision of what you want to achieve to share, this gives others something to work from.

People love to help, share their knowledge and offer advice. Lap it all up, I say. This may even be a way to get a mentor. You could also ask people about the particular networking group that you're at, how useful they have found it and so on. However, do be wary of how you take others' answers to this type of question. If they are not particularly positive about the group, it may be that their needs are not the same as yours. If they feel that the group has not been so good for them, it could be that the types of people involved in this networking group do not suit their business, or even simply that they haven't put in the effort. They may only go to every third or fourth meeting and just stand in the corner (where did you find them?). You have to be consistent and put in some effort if you're going to build up relationships.

In keeping with this idea, then, when you first start going to a particular networking group, don't go along with the attitude of "What can I get from this?" You could certainly go along with the attitude of "What can I learn?" It could also be really helpful if you could go along with the attitude of "What can I offer?" Don't worry too much if, when you're just starting out, you have no idea of what you can offer. Sometimes surprising things come up – maybe your brother-in-law is a plumber and someone you speak to happens to need a good plumber – it doesn't have to be related to you specific area, it's the fact that you're providing some kind of help that is the most important thing. Sometimes all you can offer is the possibility of future interactions, and that's okay.

When you do have interactions that you find fruitful, following up is essential to developing the relationship. This may seem obvious, but not everyone does it, and you need to be persistent and consistent. With the amount of email that everyone gets these days, you probably want to follow up with more than just "Hey, it was nice to meet you. See you at the next event." If your conversation was quite juicy, you might want to suggest meeting up for a coffee to continue the conversation, or else you might just want to say how interesting you found them and what they do and that you look forward to hearing more about them at the next event.

You could suggest a book or perhaps a TED talk that you think might interest them but, again, we are all so busy and all have access to so much information that it is likely that they're already aware of your suggestion – or something similar to it. Being told of something that you already know about can be annoying (I admit to having been on both sides of this situation!) depending on the relative experience of the two people involved (i.e., it is more acceptable for the more experienced person to suggest something to the less experienced person than the other way around).

Once you are more used to networking and have one or more established networking groups where you are becoming known for what you do, you can start to be more discerning about where you focus your networking efforts and what you see as the most effective use of your time with these groups. You should still always keep in mind the first key of building relationships – think about what you can give, first – but, as your business or ideas for your new career develop, you will have more clarity around what you want to and can achieve through your various networks. This includes what you can give back, which is a big part of building relationships. I have found that joining committees very early on can help to accelerate the building of relationships. This is a great way to immediately start giving back and others will see this which gives you a certain amount of kudos and standing.

So, the first key to networking is building relationships. The second key is persistence. And you have to be persistent to build relationships. If you remember nothing else about networking, remembering these two keys will go a long way to your success.

### What Makes You Special?

I have to admit that this question always stumped me when I first started my business. I didn't see myself as particularly special at all. Its sibling is "Why would a potential client come to you rather than someone else?" Initially, my (silent) response was, "I don't think they should – I'm just new at this. If I was in their shoes, I'd go to someone more experienced!" Actually, I might as well have said this out loud, as what I usually said was along the lines of, "I'm still working on that..."

One thing you need, to be able to answer this question, is to actually know your competition. Who are they? What do they do? What makes them different or stand out? Then you can find out where the gaps are and which ones you may fill. Again, the good old internet comes to the rescue in a big way with this. The most obvious way to start researching your competition is by looking at their webpages.

## Pause for Thought #15: Checking Out the Competition

Your next task is to check out your competition. For this *Pause for Thought* you may be better off taking notes electronically rather than with pen and paper because there will likely be more information to take account of, including links such as webpage addresses and so on which you will want to be able to just click on later. You may want to start a spreadsheet and have a separate row for each competitor, or even a separate worksheet, depending on what and how much information you'll be noting.

- Put into your favourite search engine whichever terms you think are most appropriate for your business. Don't forget to include locality if this is appropriate.

Check out the top 5-10 listings that come up and keep in mind the following questions when checking them out:

- What information do they have on their webpage?
    - How big are they?
    - How many employees do they have?
    - How long have they been in business?
- What information do they *not* have?
- What are their qualifications and/or background?
    - Have they always been in this business or have they switched careers?
    - How might this advantage them?
    - How might this disadvantage them?
- What is their niche?
- Do they have any special offers?
- If you're in a service industry, do they offer any products?
- If you're in a "product" industry (maybe you make beeswax candles), do they offer any services?
- Also see if you can work out what it is about their website that has enabled them to show up at the top of the listings.

You may not be able to find answers to some of these questions – and that's good information to have, too. One of the best things about checking out the competition is that it can give you some great ideas for yourself as well – including what you do *not* want to do or be known for.

You could also contact some of the people in the same business as you and ask to meet up with them in person. You should focus on people who are doing something as close to what you want to do as possible. They are then likely to have come across issues that you are likely to come across, and will be able to give you more targeted advice. While some people may be wary of speaking with someone who they see as future competition, those with good business sense will understand the potential opportunities that such a meeting presents. For a start, they get to check you out as well! Then there is always the possibility for joint ventures in the future, referring clients to each other, someone to brainstorm with, or even just having a sympathetic ear.

It is always nice – and reassuring – to hear that the "problems" you're having in your business are not special to you! You may even be able to "apprentice" with one or more of these people. Even if you have to do it for free, the experience you gain will be enormously beneficial.

I have met many wonderful people doing similar work to me. At the very least I feel renewed enthusiasm after chatting with someone else who understands what I am doing and why, because they are on the same path. Such people have given me some of the best advice when I have really needed it. For example, I was telling one associate about all of the things I was currently involved in and what I really wanted to spend my time doing (writing and speaking). She very kindly pointed out that it seemed that I was spreading myself too thin and that I should only focus on those activities that would put me further along the path to being able to do what I wanted to do full-time. I took her advice and started focussing on speaking rather than coaching and got three jobs in a very short time, not having had any previously.

While this fantastic piece of advice may appear to be obvious, it sometimes takes someone else pointing out the obvious for you to see it. It is too easy to get caught up in being busy and trying to take advantage of every apparent opportunity. A sympathetic and wise ear can make all the difference.

### *Pause for Thought #16: Marking Out Your Territory*

Once you've done some homework on what others are doing in your field, and you have a good feel for who is doing what and how, it is then much easier for you to answer some questions about yourself. Sit yourself down and start focussing on wonderful you. Some of the questions you need to be asking yourself are:

- What are my strengths and weaknesses?
- What are my points of credibility?
- What opportunities are there?
- What skills do I have? (Write as many as you can think of, even if they don't seem relevant just now).
- What skills do I need to develop?
- What is it best for me to pay *someone else* to do?
- Are there any gaps in the market? (location, client-type, cost level, etc.)
- What hours do I want to work?
- How much do I want to be earning?
- How big do I want my business to be? Do I want/need to have staff?

You can approach these questions in at least two different ways. You could start with your list of what you like about what others in your business do and look at how you would approach doing those things, or you could just approach them cold, purely focussing on what you have to offer, without reference to anyone else. Using both of these approaches will give you a greater breadth of ideas and possibilities. They say that creativity occurs when two seemingly disparate ideas or concepts are brought together in new ways.

If, like me, you felt that you had little tangible credibility in your newly chosen area, you might consider writing a book. While I didn't have much in the way of formal qualifications in the personal development area, I had attended a lot of courses and seminars, read a lot of books, listened to a lot of audio, and watched a lot of videos. In short, I had a lot of knowledge and experience; I just didn't have any tangible proof of the veracity of this knowledge and experience. Writing a book can help you to establish yourself as an expert in your area.

There are many other things you can do as well, particularly with respect to your web presence, such as YouTube videos and a blog. There are plenty of great books (and YouTube videos and blogs!) available that go into great detail about the best way to go about these things. If you do decide to write a book, I do recommend getting a book-writing coach. They will help to keep you on track, give you great feedback and help you with the technical side of writing a book, including publishing options, and so on.

## What Other Help is Out There?

Many cities provide free or very cheap advice, including full-day or half-day workshops and individual mentoring to help start-up businesses. This includes help with business plans. They can also recommend professionals who help start-up businesses, from accountants and lawyers to web designers. Having a great team around you will be a great boost to your success. Many local, state and even federal governments also have grant schemes available for start-ups, some of which can be quite generous.

You should also find out what professional bodies exist in your area of business. They can provide more targeted advice, particularly on any regulations you need to adhere to as well as accreditations.

As we discussed in the previous chapter, it is important to keep up your exposure to motivational ideas. At the very least spend fifteen minutes a day reading a motivational book, watching a motivational video, or listening to a motivational audio. Ideally, get yourself a coach, someone to understand where you are and be outside of your business to give a different – and non-emotionally attached – perspective, and to keep you accountable.

### Success Stories – Janine Allis, Boost Juice Founder[3]

Janine Allis is the founder of the successful franchise company, Boost Juice. She started it in her kitchen. It was not, however, her first attempt at entrepreneurialism. She had tried a couple of other ideas, including a juice business in Melbourne, before successfully launching Boost Juice in Adelaide. The idea came from seeing how well juices were doing in America while she was on holiday there. But this was not her background – she had previously been a film marketer, amongst other things.

What is clear is that she worked exceedingly hard and long hours. She was observant, taking notice of the things that would make a difference in her business and those that affected it. When she first found a potential shop location in Adelaide, she had a family member sit outside the shop location

---

3   Details taken from Kate Mills, 2011, "The Tenacious Mrs Allis", BRW Feb 10-16, pp. 20-22.

counting the number of people who went by and taking note of their gender and age[4].

Once established, she discovered a drop-off in sales in winter. However, her approach of replacing juices with soups didn't really help because Boost Juice was known for juices and customers don't necessarily make the identification leap. So this was a great lesson in market perspectives, understanding, and brand associations.

She also came to understand that in retail, because the margins are quite small, it is the volume of sales that is the key to maintaining the bottom line, so anything that could increase sales was a focus. Complementary to that, anything that could save money, even small things, was done, such as swapping from colour printing to black and white. She also understood that to give the customer what they wanted, it was necessary to ask them. To ask them, she made sure that there was a guarantee with the products, so that she had an easy way to get customer feedback, when customers made use of this guarantee.

## Chapter 10 Review

You need to get a balance between taking your time and being patient with your new business so that you make decisions for the right reasons, and taking it too easy so that you never get your business off the ground. One valuable piece of advice I was given a few years ago was to not leave your current job until you are reasonably well set up for the future. This could include a redundancy pay-out, voluntary or otherwise, or making sure that you have a few clients lined up, or even on the go, prior to leaving your current job.

Having enough cash on hand to see you through at least six months is a good idea, too – so start saving now! Also see the tips in the previous chapter on achieving financial independence. Going through the above exercises, getting yourself out networking, even if you don't feel like you've got much to say yet, and making contact with people who can help you will get you a long way towards being ready to branch out on your dream life, following your passion.

---

4   Michelle Hammond, 2012, "Boost Juice opens 200th Aussie store – three tips from founder Janine Allis" Startup Smart, 7th November. http://www.startupsmart.com.au/franchising/becoming-a-franchisor/boost-juice-opens-200th-aussie-store-three-tips-from-founder-janine-allis/201211078104.html

# Chapter 11

# Living Your Passion Now

*"There is no passion to be found in playing small – in settling for a life that is less than the one you are capable of living."*

NELSON MANDELA

There are many, many ways to live your passion. It is possible that, while you will almost certainly have a few or even many ideas from this book, it may take some time for you to get things established in a way that will financially support you into the future, even if you start developing the most perfect business plan right this second. So, what do you do in the meantime to keep the ball rolling? There is no reason why you can't start living your passion, at least in some small way, right away.

In this chapter, we will look at the many possible ways in which you can incorporate your passion into your home or personal life and into your current work life. To help you to get the most out of this chapter, we're going to jump straight into a *Pause for Thought* exercise to give you some ideas to work with.

### *Pause for Thought #17: What Can I Do Right Now?*

Get out your friendly paper and pen and have a go at answering the following questions. Your answers may or may not relate to your passion, but keep it in mind. Be as realistic as you can – particularly for the first couple of questions. You may be surprised to realise how much you actually *do* have control over in your life. And don't be bashful about what you're really gifted at. Remember, you're doing this for you. It doesn't matter at all what anyone else thinks or believes. And they don't have to see what you write, unless you let them! So, go crazy with your answers below. Let it all flow out. You will be surprised at the new perspective you have on what's possible, once you've finished answering these questions!

- What do you have control over? (You could end this sentence with "in your life" or "in the world" if either of these gets the ideas flowing more readily for you.)
- What do you not have control over? (Try to be relevant here. For example, I would wholeheartedly agree that you don't have control over the cycle of the moon, but knowing that won't shed too much light on how you can incorporate your passion into your life right now.)
- What are your skills? This can include those skills that you use in your job and those that you use elsewhere, or even those that may have been latent for a while.
- Given your skills, knowledge, experience and passions, and the nature of your employer, how can you be most effectively utilized by your employer?
- What can you negotiate about your current circumstances? People you could negotiate with include your employer, colleagues, friends or other business owners.

## Using Your Workplace as a Starting Point

Most of us spend a goodly amount of our waking hours working at a "job". If we're honest with ourselves, we work at this job largely to pay the bills. This, then, is potentially a high-leverage place to start looking for ways to incorporate your passion into your life. If you did the *Pause for Thought* reflection, above, you will have come up with some ideas that you could possibly incorporate into your current job right now, or with just a little bit of thought and strategy. As you read Ella's story, next, see if you can substitute any of her story details for your own and start creating your own "living your passion in your current workplace" story.

## Ella's Story

Ella diligently worked her way through the *Pause for Thought* exercises in this book and discovered that her passion was working creatively with flowers. She began bringing fresh flowers into work once a week, which she artistically arranged herself and kept on her desk. Initially, people simply commented on the arrangements and, each time someone did, she took the opportunity to let them know that she had done them herself. After some time, this evolved to people asking her if she did arrangements for others. Within a couple of months, she had done flowers for the wedding of a colleague's daughter, and a birthday bouquet for another colleague's wife.

Note that it doesn't hurt to start with giving discounts or even providing your services for free as we discussed earlier. This should only be for a short time, and should be to allow you to get some experience and confidence – and, very importantly, testimonials. However, it's probably a good idea to avoid being out-of-pocket yourself. If it's just a few dollars, like a cup of coffee, as you provide free coaching, say, it's probably not a big deal, but when your service involves materials, such as flowers, it's definitely not unreasonable to expect even your practice clients to pay for these. Anyway, this is a call for you to make according to your personal circumstances.

Back to Ella. About six months after Ella started bringing in her arrangements, her boss asked if she would do an arrangement of silk flowers for the office reception area. Her boss insisted on paying full rates and even paid for simple business cards for her to put next to the flowers to give to visiting clients who admired her work. She was able to take pictures of all of these opportunities to use as examples on a simple website that she was able to develop for free. (There are plenty of free website platforms available, such as Weebly and WordPress.)

After about a year, Ella was getting so much work, she was able to go part-time on her office job and also work part-time on her flower arranging business. Ella's boss hired another person to job-share with Ella, which worked well for her employer because Ella was still there to train them so that the transition would be smooth when Ella eventually left to pursue her own business full-time.

Another option, particularly if your passion is something related to relaxation or exercise, something that will encourage people out of their offices, is to run lunchtime activities. For example, if you are into yoga or meditation, you could start running classes at lunchtime for your colleagues. You could either run them for free or negotiate a price with your employer. If you want to charge, you'll need to develop a proposal which can show them how your class will benefit them, say, with respect to productivity. There are statistics available about how much more productive people are after a session of yoga or meditation.

This approach could also be adapted to other artistic or craft type passions and other workplace types. Do use your judgement, though, and do discuss it with your supervisor or boss if you think there might be any issues. And don't be disheartened or take it personally if your boss doesn't wish to use your handiwork in their office. They may just have a different idea for the look and feel of their business that doesn't match with what you're offering, and that is their prerogative and absolutely no reflection on your talent! (Though it might be a reflection on their taste – but I will leave that for you to decide!)

### What if My Passion is Outside but My Job is Inside?

Now, what if your passion isn't so easily adaptable to your current job? For example, what if your passion is to be a sports coach and you work at a desk job? You'll need to work out what level you'd like to be coaching at. Would coaching a children's team satisfy you, or are you dreaming big – and you want to coach a national or even an Olympic team? You'll also need to know what kind of qualifications you'll require, if any. For a children's team, they might be so desperate that they'll take anyone. (So they'll be thrilled to have someone of your calibre!) Maybe you could start with getting some colleagues into a friendly lunchtime competition of whichever sport it is that you fancy. You could include one day of training. If your company isn't big enough for more than one team, you could find other nearby companies to compete with.

For more senior teams, you'll almost certainly need to work your way up, so you'll need to show some experience, some success and some qualifications. You can almost certainly study for your qualifications while you're still working. There are so many distance, or online, courses available these days, and they don't have the same stigma as they used to because of the quality and availability of information, and its presentation, afforded by the internet. If you're really serious and looking at doing, say, a sports science degree, you may even want to consider doing it full-time, if you can afford it. Are you eligible for a scholarship?

You could also look at volunteering at the major clubs in the sport. You never know – it could be a backdoor way into coaching. After all, how often have you heard the saying "It's not what you know but who you know."

## What if My Boss Isn't Quite So Understanding?

Ella's story would work well in a workplace where employees are encouraged to explore their talents or where it is understood and even expected that employees will move on, such as in general clerical, retail or labour positions that require little skill and where new employees are not difficult to find, nor expensive to train. However, this is not always going to be the case, and particularly not for jobs that require greater levels of skill. Often it will be best to keep your passion separate from your day job as you get established.

You don't necessarily have to keep it hidden; it could be seen as a hobby, for example. And, obviously, you don't want to jeopardise your current job while you are still ramping up your fledgling business or skills. With respect to your employer, of course you don't want to leave them in the lurch, either. But any decent, thinking employer would rather have employees who enjoy their jobs. Employees who enjoy their jobs are generally going to be much more productive than those who don't and will probably make the workplace more enjoyable and productive for everyone. Employees who don't enjoy their jobs just bring everyone down (I bet you've had some people like this in your workplace at some point – maybe it's even been you!)

If you are feeling guilty about being secretive about wanting to leave to pursue your dream, remember that you have an employment contract that spells out what notice you are required to give. This contract will have been determined in both the interests of you and your employer. When things are not working for an employer, they will lay off employees. This is pretty much what you will be doing when you leave your employer to follow your dream. You wouldn't be leaving them if working for them was working for you.

It is helpful to think of yourself as a business or corporation which is in the business of being the best *you* that you can be. Let's call your business *Your Business*. The relationship between any employer and employee is, at its simplest, a trade partnership. These days it tends to be that one partner provides a manual or cerebral service and the other provides cash. However, which is the "employer" and which is the "employee"? It is equally valid to think of you "employing" the business that you are currently working in.

*Your Business* is employing them to provide you with a service you need, which is the provision of cash. In return, you are paying them with the provision of a service. When you no longer require their cash service, it is necessary to dissolve the trade partnership and, sadly, make them redundant. So, if you do feel more of an obligation to your employer than is indicated by your contract, remember it is your life and you actually have an obligation to yourself to make the most of your life that you can – no one else can, or will! – do that for you. By all means, offer to give more notice than is in your contract, but remember that it has been an equal trade.

### Use Your Current Activities and Networks as a Starting Point

So, what if you are in the position that it just isn't possible to explore your passion in your current job the way Ella did? Well, hopefully you have activities and or networks outside of your day job which can provide opportunities. And, if you haven't, it is fairly easy to create some. The first thing you'll need to consider is your skill levels. It could be that you have had a burning passion to create beautiful wooden furniture, but you've never so much as hammered in a nail in your life. Obviously, you'll need to get some tuition.

You could start by buying some books and trying it yourself, but there is nothing like getting advice from a seasoned professional. This can save you a lot of time, money, and effort making little – and big – mistakes that an experienced craftsperson can steer you around. Most cities and towns have adult education classes on just about anything you can think of and these are usually very reasonably priced. There are also trade schools that offer diplomas and certificates.

Once you have developed your skills somewhat, or if they are already developed, you could approach businesses working in that area and offer to work for them for free for a few hours each weekend. Remember that we are assuming that you're not leaving your current job at this stage. There's no reason why you couldn't ask to be paid but you are more likely to be taken on if you do it voluntarily. The main thing at this stage is to get some experience and exposure and start increasing your visibility in the appropriate networks. If you do a good job, the business that you're working for, for free, may offer you paid employment, or at least recommend your work to others. You will also almost certainly begin developing your own list of contacts in the field, or potential future customers, clients or employers.

I recently met a woman at a networking event who, when she was newly married, had been looking for beautiful furniture to furnish her house with. She found it all too expensive for her budget and someone suggested to her that she learn how to make it herself. So, she found and enrolled in a woodworking class. It turned out she had a real talent for it. After just six months of classes, the instructor asked her if she would like to do some teaching herself. Doing so, of course, ensured that she got even better at it, which led to her starting her own business, which she ran successfully for more than 20 years.

If you are at the stage that you're relatively expert in your passion, you can go straight into developing and expanding, or even utilising, your networks. Work out what it is that you want to offer. Will you be creating a product or a service? If it is a product, is it the kind of product that can be mass produced and sold to many different customers, such as a training program, or is it the kind of product that is only ever a once off and that needs to be tailored to each new client, such as custom-made furniture or quilts. If it is a service, is it suitable for one-on-one clients, businesses, or one-to-many such as in workshops or seminars?

Once you have an idea of what service or product you want to provide, develop your elevator pitch (there are many free resources on the internet that can help you with this) and start networking. Places that may be useful to you include local markets, chambers of commerce, meetup[5] groups and national or local associations in your field of interest. Try putting different phrases in your favourite search engine, such as "business networking <your city>" (e.g. "business networking Sydney") or "<your passion> association <your city/state>" (e.g. "woodworking association Melbourne").

### Expanding Your Job or Creating a Whole New One Without Leaving Your Employer

What if your passion is more closely related to your job? There may be potential for incorporating it into your job or convincing your boss to expand the business, possibly even with you at the helm of the new venture.

---

5    Meetup, http://www.meetup.com, is an online, worldwide organisation in which people can create their own special interest groups for others to join, and advertise events and in-person get-togethers.

## Leila's Story

Leila's passion was developing the graphics for computer games and she worked for an IT company. Unfortunately, when Leila was studying for her computer science degree, there was only one subject available on computer graphics which didn't anywhere near cover all of the techniques available, let alone give the students any depth of knowledge in any particular one.

Leila had been involved in a number of projects for her company over the previous five years. She had noticed that they were asking for more and more sophisticated graphics in their IT solutions. The company did not have the expertise required but had always been able to talk the clients out of the sophisticated graphics by emphasizing the extra cost and time it would take to include such features versus the actual tangible gains or advantages of including them. However, it was clear that the market was hankering for more sophisticated graphics and the company was in danger of being left behind, or losing future projects, if they didn't address this skill deficiency.

So, Leila did some market research and found that it would be more effective for the company to allow existing employees to improve their skills in this area than taking on new graduates or hiring experienced graphics programmers who were in great demand. She determined that it would still take a few years before the company would really have to be proficient in sophisticated graphics, giving them time to have a few people trained. This way, they would have employees who knew the company well, and who had experience and good relationships with existing clients, giving them an edge over bringing in new people.

Leila's plan was convincing enough that her company agreed to pay for her and two others to get further qualifications in computer graphics, with the agreement that they would stay on in the company for two years after they had completed their new qualifications, or else pay a certain sum of money to the company, depending on how soon they left before the two years was up. Once she had completed her qualifications, Leila was put in charge of the new computer graphics design team with a nice pay rise to go along with it.

If you do have a bit of an entrepreneurial spirit, and it is likely that you do if you are reading this book, then there are plenty of possibilities for coming up with new ideas that both allow you to indulge your passion and create more business opportunities for your employer. You just need to get a bit creative.

## Dominic's Story

Dominic was a 30-year old bank employee. He did well in year 12, but hadn't particularly wanted to go to university upon leaving school. He was more interested in earning some money, living it up a little, and seeing some of the world. He had been with the bank for 11 years where he had done well, career-wise, working his way to be a senior commercial loans consultant. However, Dominic's passion was to be a property developer. He didn't want to be just any property developer, he wanted to develop environmentally-sustainable homes with solar panels, solar hot water, composting toilets, passive solar design and natural materials.

He didn't yet feel confident enough to go out on his own, so he began deliberately seeking established property developers who were either interested in doing the same thing, and offering them great deals to purchase their loans through him. He turned his bank branch into the go-to bank for "green" property developers, and buyers looking for really sustainable homes. Because it is generally people who are better educated and with higher incomes who consider sustainable houses, this was a really great niche for him to tap into and he increased his branch's lending profits by 20% in two years.

Another alternative, if you're not ready to branch out on your own, and if you can't find an effective outlet for your passion with your current employer, is to approach other employers or businesses. If Leila hadn't been able to convince her own employer of the benefits of branching into sophisticated computer graphics, she could have altered her arguments slightly, so that they didn't rely on training current employees, and approached other IT companies instead.

## *Starting Your Own Blog*

Another possibility, which would fit in with all of the options above, is to start your own blog on the subject of your passion. There are various ways to make money from this, such as Google AdSense (allowing advertisements on your webpage), selling products related to your passion by being an affiliate (companies like Amazon and Clickbank allow you to do this, but there are plenty of others as well) or developing and selling your own products. But the biggest plus of having a blog is establishing yourself as an expert.

To get the most out of having a blog you'll need to make sure you're getting plenty of visitors (known as traffic) to your site. There are plenty of websites that give you tips on how to do this but a few starting points include:

- Commenting on others' blogs and user forums to get your name known and to establish yourself as an authority or go-to person in the field;
- Paid advertising such as with Google AdWords or on Facebook;
- Ask other bloggers in your field with a strong following to guest blog for you;
- Implement search engine optimization (SEO) techniques to get your blog at the top of the search engine rankings for appropriate search words and phrases. (It can take three to six months for your site to move up the rankings in the search engines, so be patient.)

Just as a warning, don't copy verbatim what is on others' sites. Similarly, don't write one blog article and then publish it in several places. You'll need to change it somewhat. One suggestion I have come across is to read through your article, leave it for five minutes and then try to write it again. You won't need to learn new content, but it won't be identical to your original article. The reason for making sure that you have original content is that the search engines look for copy-cats. They know who published the content first and they will penalise you for not being the original by lowering your search ranking or possibly even removing you from their pages altogether. Google, in particular, is striving for site visitors to have a "great experience" when they visit any website that Google ranks highly. A great experience includes original content.

You could also develop your own products to sell on your blog. Depending on your passion, this could be books, audio or video programs with workbooks, webinars, live seminars, mastermind groups, or one-to-one coaching. You don't need to have all of these at once; it will take time. And, the best way to develop and sell products is to work out what kinds of products you'd like to sell, give them a name and have a few dot points around what you would like the content to be and *then* market it on your blog. Once people start buying, *then* you develop the full content. If no one is buying then you haven't wasted your time developing something that no one wants. If people are buying, you'll have a great incentive to get it done!

This is by no means meant to be an exhaustive list of ways to make money from, or establish your name with, a blog. And it can be more difficult to make money from a blog than many will let on. However, it can be a great way to get your name out there, to get a feel for what interests others and to learn more about the area you are passionate about. They say that nothing helps you to learn something like having to teach it. You can think of your blog that way. If you want to be taken seriously and seen as an expert, you are going to have to make sure that what is in your blog is relevant, accurate and interesting. In other words, you will be teaching others about your passion. You'll have to do some research to make sure you get your facts right, that you can back up what you say, and that you're up-to-date.

Meetup groups were mentioned above as a good place for networking. You could also start your own meetup group. If you have enough skills, the purpose of this could be to teach others your craft or else it could be a mutual interest group where you all get together to talk about your passion and share ideas. There is the possibility of making some money from meetup groups, but you do have to check their rules carefully. I once tried creating a meetup group for a workshop I was running, because their rules stated that you could create one for a class, which I figured was the same thing. However, it seems, someone complained that my use was inappropriate, so that meetup group was shut down. At least I got my money back.

## *Social Media*

Another option, whether you decide to start your own blog or your own webpage, or not, is to use social media. Examples include: Facebook, LinkedIn, Twitter, Pinterest, and Instagram. They each have their own strengths and weaknesses. Generally, they are about building a following and getting yourself known as an expert in your area of interest. They are also a great way to reach a wide variety of people and funnel them onto your webpage (by including links to it), where you can really interest them in what you have to offer.

While there are plenty of how-to posts on the web, we'll just run quickly through how you can best use some of these platforms. Facebook is relatively casual. It allows you to amass followers. The trick is to be consistent with your posts and to engage your audience. The more you engage them, the more likely they are to see your posts in their newsfeed. If people haven't been engaging with your posts (clicking on them, liking, commenting on, or sharing them), your posts become less likely to show up in their newsfeeds, which means they'll forget about you and won't be checking out your webpage any time soon.

You want to be posting something every day and doing it in such a way that people engage. You can do this by giving them a call to action such as: "Like if you agree", "Share if this is important to you", or "Let us know what you think by leaving a comment." Facebook is really about building a community.

LinkedIn is more business-oriented. This is where your focus is more on establishing yourself as an expert in your area. You can do this by commenting on others' posts and by joining some of the many groups and being a regular contributor to these. Don't leave ridiculously long tomes as comments, but don't just write "I agree with Fred" either. Write enough to establish your credibility – and maybe inspire – but not so much that you are seen as a raving bore.

With Twitter, you would ideally be putting out several tweets a day. As this can be quite time-consuming, one way to do this is to write a whole bunch at the beginning of the day, or even the beginning of the week and schedule them throughout the day/week. You can do this via programs like Hootsuite or Buffer, which will send the same post to several platforms of your choosing.

The real value with Twitter, though, is its immediacy and timeliness. That is, it is for letting people know what you are up to *right now*, this instant. Because you are limited with the length of your message, others are more likely to read the whole thing. Of course, there are all the jokes about people tweeting when they're on the loo and, hey, if this fits in with your business, who am I to tell you not to go there? However, I would save it for things like if you had a great meeting with a client or if you saw or read something really interesting. It is to give an impression of movement, of things happening in your world – particularly as it relates to your business. People want to work with people who are going places, who have energy. Twitter can help you to express how your business is moving.

## Chapter 11 Review

You have a passion and you want to centre your life around it. This may not be possible right this instant but there are many, many things you can do to get yourself started towards this dream. So, what is possible right this instant is taking at least one action to get you going. You know what it is. Or, if you don't it's because you've actually got several to choose from and you're not sure which one to start with. You know what? It doesn't matter! Choose one. Do it. Choose another one. Do that. Now you're getting the hang of it, you're in the swing of it. Keep going until you've exhausted your list.

Actually, I'll bet that once you get started, you'll just keep adding to the possibilities. So as not to overwhelm yourself and burn yourself out, I suggest you make up a schedule over the next week or two (depending on how many you have!) for doing two or three action items a day. Do more if you like, but make sure it is manageable over time. You may also want to think about what other things you can spend less – or no – time doing, in future. For example, how many hours of television do you watch every day? Or how much time do you spend (waste!) on Facebook? Maybe, just maybe, you could be cutting these back a titch.

Just in case you're really stuck – and I can't imagine you are if you've been diligently doing all of the *Pause for Thought* reflections throughout the book – but, just in case, here are a couple of suggestions. Brainstorm a blog title and register the web address for it. For example, if your name is Carolyn, it could be as simple as "Carolyn's Blog" at www.carolynsblog.com. Or you could start writing down some book chapter and dot point content ideas. Hop to it!

# Chapter 12

# Seeing It Through

*"The wise man does at once what the fool does finally."*

BALTASAR GRACIAN

In our journey together in this book, we have explored: background on what makes you tick, philosophies on why certain things are the way they are in the world, reflections to move you towards clarifying your passions, tools to help you to see them in action, and practical tips for turning it all into reality. I would like to leave you with some final tools and ideas around dealing with your current environment because following your passion does not happen in a vacuum.

Regardless of how strong your feelings are for your passion, either discovered through this book, or long known, your life is currently the way it is for a reason. Your life is the way it currently is because of long and deeply-held beliefs and attitudes about yourself and how life should be. If your passion requires quite different beliefs and attitudes from these, to make it a significant or even the central part of your life, you'll need to make some changes.

Every part of your life is tied up with or dependent, in some way, upon every other part of your life. And, the trickiest, stickiest part of any part of your life is, of course, people. So, why are the people in your life a problem? You may be able to answer that very easily! Or you may be saying, "They won't be a problem, surely – everyone will want what's best for me. Once they know how passionate I am, they'll support and encourage me until I achieve it!"

You know, I agree with you on this – as long as you achieving what you want doesn't affect those people in too big a way!

If you affect other people by making changes in your life, that means that there will be changes in their lives, too – which they may not be ready for. If they're not ready, they're going to resist them (consciously or subconsciously), making it more difficult for you to make the changes you've decided you want to make. Obviously, you will get a range of responses from the people in your life, and we will talk about how to deal with the most common ones below, but you do need to be prepared for at least some resistance from someone – or even many someones – in your life. And, of course, one of the someones is very likely to be you!

## *Self-Sabotage*

It is highly likely that if you have struggled with making the changes you would like to make, that you have an underlying fear of what other unintended consequences those changes could bring. Fear leads to self-sabotage! Maybe you've struggled with even coming up with *what* changes you would like to make – a sure sign of self-sabotage! Let's look at some examples of people who want to follow their passions but they're in really interesting and well-paying jobs already. Because of their "go to school, get good marks, get a good job" programming, part of their subconscious is trying to tell them that they'd be crazy to leave, so they're in danger of never achieving it.

John is 30 and single. He doesn't have any kids, so the only person who is financially dependent on him is himself. He is an engineer. He is well-paid and has an interesting job. He manages a small team that designs efficient water systems for new houses, units and apartment buildings. The water systems utilise and recycle grey and black water, as well as make use of rainwater. The team's goal is to design systems that are totally independent of the water mains system. They get closer to their goal with each new system as they learn more and as new technologies come onto the market. They have also been helped by lobbying the local government to update their building rules around water usage and recycling.

What a great position John is in. He is good at his job. He is well-paid. His job is really interesting. And, as an added bonus, he is making a difference in the world by improving environmental practices in building. This really fits in well with his values. But, while he is good at his job, it isn't his passion. His passion is skydiving. He wants to run a skydiving school. As well as offering individual and tandem jumps for occasional thrill-seekers, he would like to develop parachute formation teams to enter competitions. He also has ideas for running team-building days for corporate clients.

So, what's the problem? Why doesn't he do it? The problem lies in the first sentence of the previous paragraph: John is in a great position. His "go to school, get good marks, get a good job" subconscious programming is telling him that he already has what he wants. Why would he risk it all for something that's so uncertain? He tells himself that he has a mortgage and can't risk losing his house. He tells himself he'll never find a girlfriend if he doesn't have a steady job. He tells himself that he should be happy with just doing his skydives on weekends. He tells himself that skydiving is really expensive and most people won't pay for it. He tells himself that starting your own business is really risky and it would be really difficult for him to consistently support a family, which he would like to have one day.

What do you think? His excuses sound pretty valid, don't they? Do you know why? Because you have the same programming as John! So, how can John overcome his programming? Well, the answers lie in this book. He needs to start taking in new ideas (changing his programming) every day through books and seminars. He could find a mentor or coach. He could join a networking group of like-minded people. And, he could start taking each of his excuse statements and look for ways to address them. The *Pause for Thought* exercises in this book would also help him move a long way towards changing his thinking and approach to his life.

Now, you might be thinking that John's situation is a wee bit simple because he doesn't have any dependants, so any changes he makes are really only going to affect him and it would be relatively easy for him once he starts getting a clear picture of how to go about it. But that's the key – getting a clear picture of how to go about it – or at least how to start.

Let's consider a more complicated situation. Consider Aubrey. Like John, she has a job that most people would consider a really good job. Aubrey is a physicist working for a government research organisation. She's paid well above the average. She has a lot of autonomy in her job, largely having the freedom to choose what she wants to research. She finds her job interesting and challenging in a good way. But she isn't passionate about it. Her true passion is yoga. She would love to teach it and, eventually, open her own school. She envisages running week- and even month-long retreats and, like John, she has some ideas for corporate customers.

However, she has a really nice house that she and her partner are paying off. They have two nice cars. They send their kids to good private schools that, while not the most expensive in town, still take a reasonable chunk out of their fortnightly pay packets. And they're able to afford to go on a family holiday overseas every couple of years. From the outside, life looks good. But Aubrey is not happy. She feels trapped. And she feels guilty because she thinks she should feel happy. She tells herself that she's being silly, that she should be grateful for what she has (which she should, regardless, but that doesn't mean that she has to keep everything the way it is forever). Then she tells herself that she can't afford to leave her job because she wouldn't be able to continue to afford the mortgage, cars, school fees, or holidays.

Now, certainly, Aubrey needs to consider her options very carefully as any changes she makes will almost certainly have a significant impact on her partner and children. But she does have options. The first thing she needs to do is to let her partner know how she is feeling and how important this is to her. Then they can start to make a plan, including prioritising the things in their life. Maybe they only need one car, or they could downgrade their cars. Maybe the overseas holidays can be put on hold for a few years. Maybe they can limit their eating out to a couple of times a month instead of a couple of times a week. Maybe Aubrey could go part-time for a while and they will only need to make minor changes until she gets her yoga business more established. They could make a family game out of finding ways to save money – but have more fun.

In fact, I think that in many ways Aubrey is in an easier position than John. If she can get her family behind her and they can work as a team, she has a ready-made support base to help her along when things aren't going so well – as, at times, they will be wont to do.

Self-sabotage can ruin the best of dreams. But if you can become aware that that is what is going on, you are in a position to do something about it, even if you're not initially sure why you would be sabotaging yourself from achieving your dream. For John and Aubrey, it was their strong programming around having a good job that prevented each of them from moving forward initially. It may be something different for you.

For you it may be enough to simply recognise that you are sabotaging yourself and then just find ways to move forward, such as the suggestions we made for John. Or else, it may be important to you to really get to the bottom of why you are sabotaging yourself. You may feel that unless you understand what's behind it, it will continue to beleaguer you in the future. It can take some time to get to the bottom of what is making you feel uneasy but, as you would have noticed from the *Pause for Thought* exercises, reflecting on a given situation is an invaluable tool.

## Other People Are Lessons

As humans, there is so much that we do not understand or know, individually and collectively. We do not have easy access to knowledge of life prior to birth nor after death. Regardless of your religious or spiritual beliefs, even if you believe that we are purely physical beings who cease to exist once the body can no longer support life, the biggest gift that you can give to yourself is to believe that everything is as it should be. What is happening in your life right now is happening because your subconscious has orchestrated it that way – simply through the strength of the connections that it has developed over the years of your life.

If you are in a situation that you really don't like, then you're going to need to find a way to respond to it that is different from the way you would usually respond – especially if you have previously been in this or similar situations. By responding in a really different way, you meet at least one of your six human needs by taking the opportunity to achieve some personal growth and make changes to the connections in your subconscious mind. If the changes are big enough and your personal growth has a big enough impact, this may be enough to stop this kind of situation appearing in your life in future. At the very least, the way you look at and respond to such situations in future will be very different.

Dealing with others' behaviours can be challenging at times and is one of the best types of opportunities for personal growth. If what they're doing is really pressing your buttons, though, it can take several goes – and a not insignificant amount of effort. It helps to realise that if your buttons are being pressed, *it is about you*. Someone else may not have their buttons pressed by this person's behaviour. So it is not about the other person's behaviour, but about your conditioning and programming. Not that this makes it easier to deal with straight away, or even soon. It just means that you have control over removing the problem – which you now know is your buttons and not their behaviour.

We all have buttons that get pressed – times when someone's behaviour irritates us, often for no obvious reason (we usually put it down to them being "difficult" – or words to that effect). It is usually a particular set of behaviours that press our buttons. They are an indication of aspects of our own characters that we have not accepted and do not like. You may have heard the saying that what we see in others is a reflection of ourselves. For example, we make assumptions about other people's motives based on what our own might be in that situation.

Carly was in charge of a particular business unit in her public service department, which was made up of three different work groups. The work of one of these groups was closely related to that of a group in a different business unit. There was a particular function that her group carried out that, upon analysing the overall functions of her business unit, she felt better fitted into the functions of the group in the other business unit. When she brought it up with the manager of the other business unit, however, they accused her of being lazy and trying to pass off workload to them. This kind of approach was just not Carly's way at all, and certainly not her intention. This was, instead, a reflection of the way the other business unit manager worked.

### Pause for Thought #18: What Presses Your Buttons?

It's time again for your trusty paper and pen. You're going to have a look at what some of your buttons might be, as indicated by the behaviours of people you know that cause you the most angst. I want you to think about a person who you often find irritating. Perhaps it is someone you work with or perhaps a member of your family.

- Can you identify one or more individual behaviours of theirs that irritate you? What are they?
- If you can't identify any particular behaviours of this person that irritate you (maybe you feel that they are irritating in general!), write down the circumstances of at least three occasions where you have felt irritated by this person's behaviour. Can you see any similarities in these occasions? Can you pin-point any particular behaviours that irritate you?
- Having identified at least one kind of behaviour in someone else that you find irritating, can you remember any times when you have behaved in this way ("No" is not a useful option here!)
  - How do you feel when you think of your behaviour at those times? If you come up with terms like "I cringe", or "I feel so embarrassed", can you recall why you behaved in that way? It could be that you hadn't been in that kind of situation many times before and you were simply copying how you had seen someone else (maybe one

of your parents) behave in similar circumstances – appropriately or not – as an automatic reaction, for example.
    - What kind of outcome were you hoping for in those situations? It is almost certain that you behaved in the ways that you did with the hope of getting a positive outcome for yourself, such as attention from someone you admired, or respect for the knowledge you displayed.
    - If you could go back and relive those situations but behave in a different way (like in the movie "About Time") what would you do differently?
- Return your focus to the person you first thought of in this exercise, and their behaviours that you identified as having irritated you in the past.
    - For each of these behaviours, write down what you think their intended outcome was.
    - Why do you think they behave in the way that they do?

Do you now have more acceptance of your own behaviour and more empathy for this person? While you may not ever be best friends with them, they may not irritate you quite so much in the future. In fact, you may even find that they disappear from your life altogether, as you have learned the lesson you needed to learn from them. At the very least, they may be around you much less often.

## Everyone Has a Positive Intention

It helps to have a belief that everyone, every single person you come across, acts in ways that have an intended positive outcome for them; something along the lines of a connection with another or a feeling of having the right to exist, which we all have as a basic need. Their behaviour may not easily reveal the intended positive outcome to others, if you don't know what to look for, but behaviour does not necessarily equal intention.

Many times you may choose to perceive someone else's behaviour negatively and even allow it to affect you negatively, say by getting angry or annoyed. However, this isn't necessary. You can choose to not be fazed at all by someone else's behaviour – at least to not take it personally. (Obviously if someone is coming at you with a machete, you probably need to act to get out of physical harm's way, but you can choose whether or not you then take their action as meaning that you deserved it.)

For example, a child may refer to another child as "four-eyes" if they wear glasses. This is most likely due to a need on the first child's part to feel significant, to experience a sense of power, most likely because they most often feel powerless themselves. Maybe they are being bullied by someone else. The glasses-wearing child clearly does not have four eyes (and it wouldn't matter if they did – this would then simply be a statement of fact!) and can only be upset by the comment if they feel insecure in themselves and take this comment as a statement of their inferiority or lack of worth.

In cases of name-calling or, more likely in the case of adults, unwarranted or unexpected criticism, we can only be upset if we believe there is some truth to it. We get upset because we secretly, way down deep in our subconscious, are afraid that we are unworthy, and deserving of the criticism – any criticism. If we are relatively secure in ourselves, unwarranted or unexpected criticism is like water off a duck's back, as the saying goes.

In fact, even if the criticism is warranted, as in constructive criticism, any offence taken on your part simply stems from your own insecurities. The great thing about this is that you can address these insecurities and effectively eliminate them. You know what the insecurity is because the other person basically told you – once you take away the fancy coating that they gave it. Obviously, if you react to being called "four-eyes", you aren't worried that you have four eyes. You're worried that you are unlovable in some way.

You can get to the core of why you're upset by asking some basic questions.

- What meaning have I given to being called "four-eyes"? *I have given it the meaning that I am different from others in an inferior way. This is undermining my need to feel significant.*
- What meaning have I given the fact that my partner is leaving me? *I have given it the meaning that I am not lovable. It is undermining my needs for certainty, and love and connection.*

If you think back to the six human needs, the intention of any particular behaviour is driven by one or more of those needs. When we perceive people as being egotistical, it is likely that they are being driven by the need to feel significant. When people are primarily driven by significance and certainty as adults, it can be because these needs were not adequately met when they were children. We are all born with an innate sense of place, of belonging, of having a right to be here.

However, if, as a baby, we are not given enough attention or enough of the right attention, as well as enough stability, these innate senses can be compromised, meaning that as we grow up, we will be constantly seeking to redress the balance. It is almost as if, until these core, self-centric needs are met, our psyches are unable to allow the more others-centric needs to be our primary drivers. They still need to be met, but they are most often not one of our driving needs.

## *Pause for Thought #19: What Message Are You Taking On?*

Are you struggling with a particular incident at present? Has someone said or implied something about you that has left you feeling a bit miffed, or even distraught? Perhaps someone cut you off in traffic this morning, or ignored you as you passed them in the corridor and you can't stop thinking about it and getting angry. If so, grab a cup of tea and your paper and pen and let's have a muddle through it and see if we can get to the real source of your angst.

- What is it that is giving you angst? Who was involved, and what did they say? Include as much detail as you can.
- Now write down on a new line, or even a new page: "What meaning have I given to X saying/doing Y about/to me?" where X and Y are your answers to the previous question. (Change the wording in this sentence as appropriate to your situation.)
- Now start writing down whatever answers come into your head. Keep writing down answers at least until you get to one that gives you a sense of "Aha!".
    - You may even want to continue after your first "Aha!", as there may be more than one aspect to your angst.
- Now, for each of your "Aha!" answers, ask yourself the following. Again, write down as many answers as you can.
    - Why might I believe this is true?
    You are looking for other incidents or times when you felt the same way. Try going back through your life, as far back as possible, to find your earliest possible memory of feeling this way.
    - Now I want you to go back through your life and come up with at least as many times when you felt the opposite. For example, if your "Aha!" is that you've realised that the meaning you've given to what this person said about you is that you're not lovable, go back through your life, starting from today, and find times when you felt loved.

When you attach a meaning like this to something someone does, or says about or to you, it can be easy to immerse yourself in it, without even being aware of the meaning. By identifying it, you are on step one of overcoming your belief in it and, by then finding examples that show that the opposite is true, it is possible to get to the roots of your original belief, pull the whole thing out and throw it onto the proverbial compost heap to grow into a belief that is much more beneficial to you.

## Who Are My Friends?

We talked at the beginning of this chapter about the possible difficulties you could face from other people in your life who may perceive that any changes you want to make will affect them negatively – fairly or not. Well, it may be that it is time for you and such people to part ways or, at least, spend less time together. The reality is that, sometimes, to move forward, to change, you need to change who you spend your time with, who you hang around with. For many people, this can understandably be a scary proposition. Let's explore this a little more.

First, what difference does it make who you hang around with? There is a saying popular in the motivational speaking world that what you earn is the average of the earnings of the five people you spend most of your time with. (Contemplate that for a second...) And remember the grey sludge that you get filled up with every day from hearing the same messages over and over because you are in the same environment every day? To get new messages, you need to change something about your everyday environment.

This doesn't mean that you have to change everything at once. No one is saying that you must immediately (or ever!) leave your marriage, or move to a new city to get away from your current set of friends. The friends you cherish the most are likely to be the ones you should be hanging on to and will have no qualms about doing so. However, if you are really serious about changing your life, it is likely that you have already identified a number of people who you would rather spend less or even no time with.

To help you to determine what beneficial changes you could make to your social circle right now, changes that you would feel comfortable making, you're going to do a short reflection exercise around your current friendships. At the end of this exercise you will know which friendships you absolutely want to keep, which you want to tone down, which are really not serving you that you will be relieved to be rid of, and what new types of friendships and associations you would now benefit from cultivating.

## Pause for Thought #20: To Friend or Not to Friend

Now, consider the following questions in relation to the people in your social circle. You can either write down a list of everyone you have reasonably regular contact with and then go through the questions for each person or else see who pops into your head most readily as you ask each question. It doesn't matter if you don't cover everyone the first time you do this. Anyone you don't think of now, you can consider when next you have contact with them.

One final thing before you start answering the social circle questions. When considering the people in your social circle, don't forget those who you don't know very well, but who you would like to get to know better. It may be that there are some new people you have met who have the growth mindset that you are trying to nurture but you may have felt intimidated by them in the past, as if you may have been dragging them down. They seem so in control of their lives, so energetic that you may have felt that they didn't have room for you or that you didn't have anything to offer them. Well, now you're really opening up to the possibilities out there, such friendships may have the chance to blossom. Okay, so now to the questions.

- *Which of the people in your social circle do you genuinely look forward to catching up with?*

    These people make you feel energised and good about yourself most, if not all, of the time. You have a lot in common and it is likely that they are also interested in bettering themselves, exploring what more life has to offer. They may have even been the inspiration for you starting or expanding your own personal development journey. These are friends you probably want to keep seeing on a regular basis. If you haven't been seeing them on a regular basis, it's time to start. Call or email them now to make a time to meet up for a chat. (Really, call or email them right now!) When you do meet, tell them about your aspirations. They are likely to be your biggest supporters. And we can all benefit from having more supporters! You never know, it may even lead to starting a business venture together.

- *Which of the people in your social circle are you okay about spending time with but, if you're honest with yourself, you do it more out of habit than desire?*

    These people may, more often than not, make you feel a bit drained after meeting with them. You may have known them since high school or even since childhood. They know you really well, and you, them. There is a feeling of being comfortable, but there is no real spark to the friendship. Your conversations are largely gossip about people you both know. If you feel like you would really, really miss them, there is no reason why you shouldn't see them ever, but maybe make it a bit less often, make the visits shorter, or wait for them to call you next time.

    If they already initiate all of your meet-ups, this is a pretty big clue that deep down, you already know that they aren't such a positive influence in your life. Before you start feeling too badly, look for any clues that indicate that they may be feeling the same way. How often they call isn't necessarily an indication. Calling often out of neediness is not a sign of true friendship or connection.

    Another possibility with the people that fit into this category, if you haven't talked to them about your ideas for expanding your life experiences, is that you could arrange to meet them in the next few days to tell them about your new venture. If they react positively, there may be a chance that they could move into the previous category. Otherwise, particularly if they fall into the group that you think are really just keeping up the friendship because they are lonely, you could introduce them to another friend or two who fall into this category and maybe they will hit it off. At least then you've done something to help them and haven't just abandoned them.

- *Which of the people in your social circle do you pretty much dread spending time with?*

    It may be that you have a great deal of respect or admiration for these people. They may be highly intelligent and articulate. But they may also be argumentative, sceptical and negative. Whether intelligent or not, if someone is constantly complaining and shooting down any ideas you have, you probably don't want to be spending time with them. It's not a good sign if you feel sapped of your energy every time you spend time with this person.

    Another type of person that can fit into this category is the person who is constantly giving you unsolicited advice on everything from your relationship ("Honestly, he is a bastard. You should find someone else.") to your dress-sense ("You really shouldn't wear so much black, it makes you look pale.") to how to get promoted in your job – particularly when they work in an entirely different field and have never been promoted themselves.

If they never listen to you, always make the conversation about themselves, or only ever communicate at a superficial level, I doubt that you're going to miss them. It's best to leave these people to their other friends. I can't imagine that they're really getting anything positive out of your friendship either, except maybe an ego boost when they think they've given you some good advice (which is generally based in their own insecurity, anyway).

If any of the above sounds harsh, remember that, apart from your children while they are growing up (and only while they are growing up – remember how old you were when you wanted your parents to stop telling you what you should do with your life…), the only person whose life you are responsible for is you. If you thought you were being a drain on someone else, would you really want that to continue? I doubt it. (And if you did, you might want to consult a good therapist.) So, why is it okay to allow someone else to be a drain on you?

You are not doing anybody any favours by being a part of them keeping themselves in a place where they are not growing, or by allowing them to keep you in a place where you are not growing. The best way that you can make the world a better place is by being the best person that you can be. And you can do that by constantly seeking out new information and experiences that will help you to grow as a person. By doing this you can be an example to others. If they are inspired to make changes of their own, great; if not, continuing the friendship in the old way was never going to help them in this way, anyway.

So, now you should have a list of the friends who are contributing to your life in a really positive way. These are the people who you should be spending most of your social time with. If you followed the instructions above, you have already made a time to meet with each one of them in the near future! And how exciting is that? You're guaranteed to be spending time with people who make you feel great!

## *Your Intimate Relationship*

Okay, so you've sorted out your friends. What about your intimate relationship? You may be lucky enough to be able to say that your partner is on the same path as you and you're confident they'll be supportive of your dream, or they already are being supportive – maybe they have been your inspiration. On the other hand, you may not be so sure how they might respond to the new, mentally and spiritually growing and expanding you.

If you're not sure how your partner will respond, the chances are that the communication in your relationship is not as good as it could be. Now, this is certainly not a relationship manual – there are plenty of great books on relationships out there – but the following ideas will at least get you started. So, the first thing you probably need to tackle is the communication. You need to be honest with yourself about how communicative and open you are with your partner, and where there might be room for improvement. Be interested in them and what they do, but don't lose yourself in the process.

Do you stop what you're doing and make a deliberate effort to welcome them when they get home, if you're the first home, or seek them out to say hello if you're second home? Or did this habit disappear long ago? Ask them every day how their day was and what they did. Don't give advice, unless they specifically ask for it, just listen. There is a saying that goes "Being listened to is so close to being loved that most people can't tell the difference." Ask them for the same in return.

If you're not sharing what you do each day, how can you possibly share what you want for a future together, especially as it will change as you both grow as people? There would almost certainly be something not right if you each wanted the same things for your future when you were 40 as you did when you were 20, or even 30. You are both going to be constantly evolving in your ideas and perspective of yourselves, each other, the world and what is possible or even desirable. The experiences that you have apart can be just as enriching for your relationship as the experiences you have together.

So you need to be constantly communicating to explore your evolving ideas together. This way, when anything really radical emerges, ideally it is still in its infancy in whichever partner's mind it sprang from and won't be as potentially threatening to the other partner as a fully-formed, planned out idea would be. At this point, you both have the opportunity to be involved in its evolution, which is important if it is something that will significantly impact on both of you.

However, if you are at the point where you have a relatively well-developed plan in your head for pursuing your passion and you haven't yet broached it with your partner, now would be a good time to do so. If your plan is quite radical and means significant changes for both of you, you may need to step carefully. While your partner may see the value in all aspects of your plan, they may also need some time to get used to the idea. After all, if your idea is quite well-developed, you've already had plenty of time to get used to it. Give them a chance to catch up.

To minimize resistance, don't give them too much to resist. In the first instance, just reveal the essential part of your idea (such as – "I think I'd like to pursue being a Cordon Bleu chef"). Even if you've already decided on the course you'd like to do, worked out a plan to afford the fees and drafted a resignation letter to your current boss, allow the discussion to evolve as your partner absorbs and accepts the implications.

On the surface this may seem manipulative, but it's really just common sense. Imagine if we presented calculus to children on their first day of school. At this point, they most likely can't even add, let alone know the concept of area (say, of a circle or even just a square), which is essential to an understanding of calculus. They would most likely claim an immediate dislike for mathematics and go and find a ball or skipping rope to play with instead. They need time to understand the fundamentals before they can move on to more complex concepts. Presenting calculus to children in this way is completely unfair to them and, actually, doing them a disservice by presenting them with something for which they have not been sufficiently prepared to tackle effectively.

And so it is if you have a particularly radical idea that you'd like to present to your partner. You've had plenty of time to develop and get used to the idea yourself. If someone had presented it to you initially, practically fully-formed, you would probably have baulked at it, too! Just because you've come up with a feasible plan doesn't mean it's the only one or that you're not open to other ideas, so it only makes sense to take it slowly when first discussing it with your partner. If you approach your partner in a slow, measured way, they will have the opportunity to consider the possibilities themselves and, you never know, they may even come up with more effective steps than you did – or you may evolve even better ideas together.

They may also reveal a burning desire for change that will equally impact on both of you, that also needs to be taken into consideration. By approaching your partner in a step-by-step fashion, you are giving both of you the opportunity to discover what a great opportunity your idea really is for the both of you. If the idea is important enough to you, to your future well-being, this is not manipulation, but a real opportunity for growth – you will know the difference, and so will your partner.

If you are having great difficulty in finding a common ground, or a way forward that you are both comfortable with, it may be worthwhile seeking some counselling – perhaps both individually and separately. The disagreement may be a symptom of deeper issues. Recall the story of Sunita and her partner. We explored the possibility that the resistance behaviours of both she and her partner were as a result of feelings of fear around loss of security. Most often, strong reactions like this come from unresolved childhood issues, which we have touched on many times throughout the book.

Once you do get to the bottom of the issues, there are, really, two possibilities; either you will be able to find a common ground and can move forward together – maybe in a completely different direction from the one that you started with, or you will decide to part ways. I am not trying to scare you. If you are both honest with how you feel and where any fears come from, parting can be amicable, with you both understanding that it is for the best for each of you. Ideally you will very quickly start looking forward to your new life and the opportunities and possibilities now open to you.

As glib as this can sound when you are in the middle of it, a heartbreaking event can often be the best thing that could happen to you. It can force you to face your fears and break out of old patterns. Remember the first time you had your heart broken? How do you feel about that now? How do you feel about the person who broke it now? I would bet that most of you are letting out a huge sigh of relief and possibly even thinking, "Yes! What on Earth was I thinking going out with them in the first place?!" Or at the very least you're realising how incompatible the two of you actually were, even if you do still harbour a bit of a torch for them. And you may even recognise all of the great things you have or have done in your life which likely wouldn't have happened if you had stayed with that person.

As I previously said, I am a strong believer in the idea that what is best for you right now is whatever you are experiencing right now. If you think of your life as being a series of experiences put in front of you to help you to grow, then the most painful and difficult experiences are often the ones that give you the opportunity to grow the most. You will know when you have grown through that experience as much as you can, because you will feel an acceptance of it. If you are still hanging on to grief, bitterness or resentment, keep working on it, you can get to acceptance – for any experience.

*Chapter 12 Review*

No matter what your passion is and whether or not you are currently living it, life is a series of lessons and opportunities for experiencing personal growth, love and connection and making a contribution. On your way to creating your ideal passionate life, there are still plenty of ways to experience or incorporate your passion. Don't let obstacles or lack of progress put you off. Just see them as opportunities for growth. You just need to have the right attitude towards them.

Self-reflection on your attitudes towards certain people can help you to move through the lessons those people are in your life to teach you. The people around you have a significant impact on your life – make sure you are surrounded by people who are going to help you along your way to your ideal, passionate life, and not hinder you.

# Conclusion

This is your life. It is not the life of anyone else. Therefore, you have total say in what you do with it. It is my belief that if you allow your understanding of the six human needs to be your guide, choosing the most appropriate drivers and focussing on the belief that life is about experiencing love and joy, you will have a passion-filled, joyous, wonderful life.

Everyone has at least one thing that they are passionate about. The trick is to find it. You may be one of those lucky people who has always been sure of what their passion is. Or, if not, it is my true wish that the ideas and reflections in this book have helped you to identify a passion or, at the very least, some things that you'd like to try out to explore their potential for being your passion.

It makes no sense to me at all for anyone to live a life that is not filled with love and joy. That so many people do, says to me that many of us have lost our way. We have forgotten what it is to be human. We don't take notice of the natural fun that children have; the delight that particularly small children see in everything new. If everyone could find just one thing to find delight in every day, I am convinced the world would be a different place.

Through this book, it is my hope that you have found a new way of looking at your life and the world around you. It is, truly, a journey in which every step is an opportunity for personal growth, love and connection and making a difference to the lives of others, as well as your own.

Don't make the mistake of thinking that you have control of your life because you have gone to school, got good grades, got a tertiary qualification and, finally, got a good job. What will you do if you lose that job, say, through an unexpected redundancy or wave of retrenchments? And, staying in a "good" job that you actually get little joy out of is a waste of your life. True control is having the resilience and resources to always be happy, regardless of the situation you find yourself in, from bankruptcy to untold wealth.

Don't make the mistake of thinking that you have to know exactly where you're going and everything you want for the rest of your life before you can even get started on making any changes. This is not how "the system" works. You can waste precious energy and time, potentially years, or even your whole life, grappling with this if you don't realise that this is just how it is. You don't have to have everything perfect in order to begin. You don't have to have everything mapped out.

For it to even be possible to have everything completely mapped out, you would have to be able to predict the future, because there will be so many unknowns that could come into play along the way due to interactions with and actions of other people. You can increase the probability of certain things happening by undertaking particular actions, but you are unlikely to be 100% right all or even most of the time. And that is part of the joy of life – being pleasantly surprised by the unexpected. This is also aligned with one of the keys to life – accepting the unwanted, or not so pleasant, unexpected. Do not judge anything that happens as good or bad. Simply accept whatever happens.

On the road to living your passion, find something to be grateful for every day. Find something to do every day that you love to do – sing, dance, or photograph a beautiful flower – or your child. Notice something to love in every person you meet, particularly, and especially, your family.

Whether or not you believe in a life's path being mapped out for (or by) you, prior to entering this life, you can still acknowledge that you are happier doing some things than others. And you will have noticed that other people enjoy doing things, and get immense pleasure from them, that you couldn't be paid enough to do.

You are at your best when you are doing things for which you don't notice the time going past you or how tired you are. You can do these activities for hours on end and be in a state of near, if not total, bliss. Some refer to it as being "in the zone", others as a feeling of oneness with their world. When undertaking such activities you feel a true sense of purpose. Make it your life's purpose to find a way to live every minute of every day like this.

# Acknowledgments

I would like to acknowledge all of the teachers and mentors I have had through my experiences in the motivational speaking world. They are too many to mention them all individually and it would be impossible to say from whom I have gleaned the most valuable advice. I have been to many, many seminars, read many, many books, listened to many, many audio recordings and watched many, many videos on various topics of personal development. I have learned something new from every single one. Sometimes it has been the same idea proposed in a different way, but it has always been useful.

I am indebted to my friends and co-mentors, Deborah Farrell and Sam Barrett, who I met on a six month NLP/coaching course. We have kept in constant contact now for more than two years, catching up over Skype at least once a month (we live in different cities, all separated by at least 1000km), supporting each other and celebrating each other's successes. Their encouragement and wise insights have kept me going through writing this book – and helped to make sure I got it completed.

My fabulous authoring mentor, Emily Gowor, has been an amazing guide throughout the process of writing this book. She is such an inspirational woman, it is difficult to not get caught up in her excitement and enthusiasm for life and realising your dreams. Her insights and thoughtful feedback have helped to shape this book in wonderful ways I could not have achieved by myself.

I would also like to thank my first life coach, Kevin Barnes, who opened me up to many ideas and possibilities in the personal development world. He inspired me through his own success stories along his own path to living his passion. He gave me a different perspective on myself, my skills, and what I had to offer that helped me to make the leap and leave a job I was comfortable in but not enjoying, to explore the possibilities beyond it.

Finally, I would like to thank my family: my parents for providing an environment where exploring your dreams was possible; and my sister and brother and their wonderful spouses, for being supportive of me and encouraging me and always just being there when I need them; and my nieces and nephews for just being their beautiful selves.

# About The Author

Dr. Haley Jones is an author and speaker who helps people clarify what their passion is and how they can fulfil it. Working with adults and children, Dr. Jones aims to change the ingrained cultural mindset that promotes financial security above personal fulfilment. Her engaging and thoughtful workshops and books cause people to reshape their thoughts towards career and money. With her sharp intellect and knowledge of wealth creation and personal development, Dr. Jones teaches practical methods for discovering and following one's true path.

A curious and spiritual child, Dr. Jones developed a strong interest in personal development and the human search for meaning. Despite this, she steered her enquiring mind towards education in maths, physics, computer science, and eventually a PhD. She worked as an electrical and electronics engineer and conducted research in telecommunications engineering. Stifled by this theoretical environment, and wanting to make a more lasting positive impact on the world, she switched to sustainable engineering. At this point, her true path became clear. She wanted to change the world, but she wanted to start at an individual level, and she wanted to do this through personal development and career fulfilment. Dr. Jones realised it is empowered, and – more importantly – happy people, who respect and care for the world they're in. After undertaking further courses in wealth creation, entrepreneurship and personal development, she made a change and has not looked back.

As a writer and presenter, Dr. Jones holds workshops in schools and for adults. She is dedicated to creating knowledge about how passive wealth can be created so that people are free to do what they love. Addressing a gap in our culture that downplays the importance of meaning in work, she shows how this is possible through the understanding of wealth creation and cash flow. With the knowledge she provides, it is easy to see how financial security and a job that you love are not mutually exclusive. Dr. Jones equips people with the tools to make better decisions and to understand the cumulative effect of the choices they have made. Those who are fortunate enough to read or hear Dr. Jones' advice, find a greater sense of freedom and ability to challenge their current mindset. While she has a spiritual basis to her work, Dr. Jones is ultimately practical and driven by proven methods. Aware of modern challenges, she has created a foolproof structure for surviving our current culture, but doing so in the most fulfilling way possible.

*"My mission is help others break free from the grey sludge of misinformation they've been fed since birth to find their real purpose,"* says Dr. Jones. *"People light up, relax, and look happier knowing that they do have a choice in what they do. Life should be fun and if you do what you love, everything else will follow."*

Dr. Jones' gentle but strong-minded approach highlights the potential outside of the standard nine-to-five box. Her booklet, *What if Money Wasn't an Issue*, is a smart guide on creating passive income, which goes to the heart of Dr. Jones' aim. Ultimately, she wants to free people from their constraints so that they can experience the joy embedded in everyday life.

www.drhaleyjones.com